NEW POETS:
WOMEN

an anthology

Edited by Terry Wetherby

Les Femmes Publishing
Millbrae, California

First Printing: March 1976
Made in the United States of America

1 2 3 4 5 6 7 8 − 80 79 78 77 76

Library of Congress Cataloging in Publication Data

Main entry under title:

New poets, women.

1. American poetry—Women authors. 2. American
poetry—20th century. I. Wetherby, Terry.
PS589.N37   811'.5'408   75—28775
ISBN 0-89087-908-7

CONTENTS

iv

Introduction

Poetry has become an in-group experience. Either as a cause or as a result of this condition, poetry is largely an inbred artistic concern, one which thrives in small groups throughout the country or in isolated individuals. Poets, generally, write for poets; poets teach and communicate with poets; poets publish and promote—among themselves—other poets. Meanwhile, poetry becomes more and more a contemporary separatist art, divided from the general readership, non-poets, at large.

Anthologies, generally, include a host of the bright young or old stars, hand-set in a galaxy on which this lost audience never is intended to set eyes. In this anthology, I have attempted to give poetry to the reading population as well as to poets. Hopefully, collections such as this —gathered without respect to "names" or prize-winners or associations—will serve as an indication of the variety of voices and concerns now being recorded in this form we call poetry. This anthology is one attempt to give a sense of scope to all readers.

Women's poetry is presented here because I believe that such work receives less attention than it should. NEW POETS: WOMEN presents poems by women who, at the time of selection, did not have a book of poetry in print. Forty-one women are represented. They speak from experiences in the ghetto, the country, suburbia, and from a variety of lifestyles, age groups, ethnic and educational backgrounds. Basic biographical data concerning each of these forty-one poets is provided.

Much is made of women's driving concerns today. This collection presents various views of those concerns and of the human condition, allowing for different "schools" and styles—an unusual approach, it seems, in current anthologies.

New voices are here and established voices reintroduced. The heretofore unpublished are back-to-back with recipients of highly respected writing grants and awards.

It is my hope that this collection speaks for itself on behalf of the most pertinent interests of poetry and of our age.

Terry Wetherby
San Francisco

PHOTO CREDITS / NEW POETS: WOMEN

POET	PHOTOGRAPHER
Chilgren, Delia	Lorraine Rorke
Koster, Gloria	Peltz
Levenberg, Diane	Layle Silbert
Marcus, Adrianne	Alonso D. Gonzalez
Moore, Rosalie	Sydney Rachel Goldstein
Payne, Gerrye	Zeese Papanikolas
Prado, Holly	David Oyster
Ryan, Margaret	Ed Voytavitch
Scott, Virginia	Jean Verthein
Silbert, Layle	Robert Lax
Yoak, Martha	Tom Schmidt

LAURA BEAUSOLEIL

ON THE BORDER OF IMPOSSIBILITY

On the border of impossibility
we always stop
there is not much more
that hands can do

Our thighs stretch out
beyond our knees
and we follow them like roads
until they too divide
and stop

Then we turn back into
the invisibility of numbers
and an alphabet
we cannot speak

It is always the same
sometimes the heart moves
and sometimes it is left
floating in the chest

LAURA BEAUSOLEIL

NIGHT OF DREAMS

1

You were lying on top of me
waving your small hand.
I was concerned about
the foreign invasion,
the tiny animals
threatening to explode my ovaries.
You gave me a rubber palate,
you said it was an interheart device
that would prevent this sort of thing
from happening. Maybe I was
reassured. I reached to touch the hole
in your buttocks and was
sucked in.

2

The street lights
are stretching like amoebae
they are trying to reach in
and read my palm
they are discussing my future
humming their voices
like refrigerators
I should get up and confirm them
but sleep more comfortable
I go on
listening to my diagnosis

3

I hear the splintering of stairs.
I hear the beads that
covered the door
where you used to live.
You with your huge breasts
and infallible IUD.

You used to say
how beautiful I was
and tell the men in the bars
that we were lovers.
We spent hours together
cutting the people we knew
up in pieces and putting them
back together as poems.
Why are you walking
around here tonight?
I know that you are in
Amsterdam. Why are you rattling
those beads?
You lived only in that house
a short while
before the child died.
You have only to get up again
and leave us all behind.

4

This situation can only be analyzed
mathematically. Just 100 feet from
the monster's eye my finger rests
on the pillow. I have one minute to get
away. My mother and father are
already breathing the poison. My friends
from high school are trying on
new dresses. My brother is eating
his fingernails. A boat will touch
the tip of the island just in time.
There will be a yard between
the wharf and the deck of the boat.
I will have to wake up and jump.

LAURA BEAUSOLEIL

SUNDAY

You were up early
out in the garden
picking the worms
off the cabbage plants.

Still naked,
when you knelt down
the sacs of skin
hung between your legs
warm and dark like fruit.

Now   sometimes
I dream about
the inside of your mouth,
or remember breakfast,
the strawberries floating in milk
like kisses.

When I see you again
I will show you
this,
a cold tongue growing in my hand
like a child.

Already
it is eating without me,
it has my memory, but
it will tell you everything.

JOANNE CASULLO

FATHER AND DAUGHTER

We tolerate closed doors by watching the sun
streak washed windows like wrinkles
till you draw the curtains manually
and cast the room in blood.

We are stained by our blindness:
your sensitivity to light,
my eagerness to need.

When you leave, car fumes creep from the garage
like kittens stalking woolen prey.
Only the holes in the cinder block breathe.

I am mistaken for others in this night
that brings its hands together
in a midnight position.
All that makes a difference is the name
that resembles mine
on the base of a bronze shoe.

JOANNE CASULLO

MISTAKEN IDENTITY

The woman dressed in half brown shoes
walked three miles around a small square area.
The tables moved closer together until
she couldn't fit. My sister divided time
in half and, forcing the tables apart, went in,
letting them snap shut behind her
like Ali Baba's rock. Only twenty men
dressed in plain clothes followed me
asking questions, needing change
of five and ten dollar bills.
My sister waited in a phone booth
closed and lit by a 40-watt memorial.

That woman, her brown shoes next to her,
had climbed onto the table. Mistaking me,
she demanded my palms be read aloud
for the good of the nation.
I moved without rest but still
the tables would not budge.

Six men wrapped in gold drapes approached,
wing-tip shoes declaring five of them
charlatans. My own sister gave up waiting,
walked past me, circled by pretending palmists,
without recognition.

TRANSLATION	*FROM*	*ORIGINAL*

Between us, a mild river
runs through underbrush,
dogs climb banks and a full moon
goes into clouds,
coming apart.
Shadows stretch to absence
where I climb a tree
and pretend to fly.

                  I

When the dogs cross over,
they stumble, feathers forced
toward me from their foaming
gums and one muscle in my leg
brings me down.
With leaves under my arms,   am
I ellipse back to the rich
mud banks and set afloat
a leaf-barge.

No sound reaches anywhere
as someone climbs that tree
where I left borrowed shoes
and a toothbrush decoy
the dogs must recognize.   escaping;
I crawl along on my belly,
never letting the barge
out of sight.

The sky: have
silver saliva
where once the moon.

I set my shoes
on my back inside
my shirt, and turn west,
counterclockwise.   escaped.

7

JOANNE CASULLO

THE SUICIDE

Before she sold her life to the asphalt,
she put things in their places,
high on the backs of steel shelves.

She took seven eggs, the bread and milk
in a brown paper bag
and set it at her neighbor's door.

When the landlord searched her apartment
he found a notebook she'd taken with her
to the windowsill.

The book explained nothing, held sketch upon sketch
of distant mountains, only triangles
when looked at closely.

DELIA CHILGREN

NIGHTWALKER

He sleeps in the next room
oblivious to my wanderings
the curve of his nakedness
a home to come back to

I am not still
but up the hall and back
silences of my slippered steps
through each abandoned room
removing myself from the scent of his sheets

I inhale lingering perfumes
the flatness of the coming day
(our days together)
the kitchen is a cove of leftovers
my thoughts are moored in

DELIA CHILGREN

LETTER TO MY FATHER

I couldn't find my playground
though I searched all afternoon, tracing
circles of steps through the park.
It is hidden away by the same them
who took away my childhood, or they
have changed it beyond recollection
in this taller, more tamed garden.
My favorite for its fuzzy sheep, fillies,
chickens, goats—a grove with merry-go-round
& train that scared me each time down the hill.
All unutterably altered,
and you dead.
(my poems found locked in your desk drawer)

Strolls in other gardens
we never had in 20 years haunt me
in the nightmare where I sleep. I ache
for our zoo afternoons
watching spindly goats rise with parental
nudging. In these six months
I've crumbled in absence of your shadow
—my steps unsteady as any zoo animal—
the park, in time, betrayed.

BIG SUR SUMMER

Coleman lantern light poses the parameter of darkness
at which boundary emerge two figures,
men of 20 or so, one taller and blonder
the other dark enough to speak night within himself:
the Big Sur coastline is a shadow across his palm

A night of strangers; bright stars mark the heavens
a cloudless heaven roof of leaves our geography:
let us speak to each other
sit at table and eat our meal
(eons and eons pass) we are done eating
(the moon has risen and multiplies on our plates)

Mountain takes shape behind my back, light
flickers to define the silences; our words seek
other terrains than this. The two men hold their
common solitude as a cape against the cold (they walk
like priests up the mountain path)
Unlike what I have known,
the color of their eyes in lantern light . . .

CATHY COLMAN

Your cheekbones live. . .

Your cheekbones live
in my drawings beside the wet leaves
and smoke in the creek night
in Idaho, the ground was soft.
when you took me
it was like turning over a rock
with a rattlesnake underneath.
our life went like that
when you panic
the venom goes quicker to the heart.

bird, ghost-of-bird
the earth won't remember.

we were in the waiting forest.
the sky was green there.
I woke with wild-colored
flowers by my head.

the deer almost ate
the hunters ate her.
white sky before sun
the photograph
before it's a photograph.

I trust to you, light.
I drank you as my own reflection.
Keep me drunk
in the snake-bone dark
of your white.

AFTER SWIMMING IN THE PACIFIC

you said it was just sex, we had
I want to point to a mirror and say
see that girl in there
she is a book with many fine illustrations
a landscape you want to hold
hold me.

this is not something you can ask
sometimes.

in the ocean each wave is death
until I come up breathing.
it is so big
when I swallow it
I get eaten.

if I were an eagle
I'd know the meaning of shadow
the rabbit outruns
his shadow
crazy in whiteness.

I cannot come down.
I am pinned to the sky
in a dream
where my words
fall like snow.

you are not curious.
it is only winter.

CATHY COLMAN

FOX COURT, WINTER

safety pin on the floor
is 7:30.
not one real flower in the house.
at night, I watch the stars through the skylight
we are still
together.
in the morning, clouds go
smoke fast
I am at sea
in the earth.

unused portion
of the brain's seed
the pinecone would
be a flower.
it is my mouth
that hungers
waking, woman, so what.
even the light
poses.
voice said: the world is used
you are too good

angel with cool hands
has gone into the locked dream
heart left the camellia
shrinking in the night
when small things
are supposed
to grow.

ELLEN COONEY

so you dance with me. . .

so you dance with me
in your arms
I am leaden at first
I fear you
mother of fire
I fear you
mother of dance
time bleeds
music bleeds
it won't be long enough
then your smile
soft gentle and melodious
it tucks me in
under warm blankets
it quenches my thirst
your strength flows through me
thick water
much stronger than sea
it quenches my thirst

ELLEN COONEY

From four walls of. . .

From four walls of
ivory
a room thick with tired palms
she receives the honors
of her court by day
: a virgin in white
almost marble haired
languid and ancient on a cream colored throne
a laurel wreath nearby
several
hundred years old and abandoned by a slave
who once brought her juleps
and cool green velvet
pillows for her head

MONDAY NIGHT IN WINTER

my sister
we are lying in a large bed by the sea
under white blankets
we are little again
our parents are in another country
nothing matters but the sea
cradles and rocks us
there is no blood on the sheets
our room is tiny
in the refrigerator there is nothing but milk
a white moon guards us through the window
as we sleep in each other's arms

TOI DERRICOTTE

BOXES

a man builds boxes
one
inside
another

he wants to live in the last box

he is shrinking

the walls
get thin
as onion skin

he knocks off in the crotch of a corner

strata of dead air
mother him

TOI DERRICOTTE

DOLL POEM

doll is sitting in a box
she watches me
with two gray eyes
i take the top off
& look at her
she is wearing rubbers
to keep her feet dry
she is wearing eyeglasses
2 inches thick
she has padding on her soft behind
she is wearing excuses
all over
she is carrying threads
& buttons
she is a good hausfrau
prepared for all necessities
with kleenex
& kotex
& pencils
& lifesavers
& a boy doll with a wedding ring
she has lists as endless as dirt
 a grocery list
 a christmas list
 a wine list
 a list of sins
 a list of movies
 a list of friends
her lists grow up
& eat lbs. of other lists

she is clean   clean   clean
she is rabbit quick
she copulates with ideas
she is good as gold
she is desirable as a tooth fairy
she is the color of permanent
teeth
ask her her name
& turn her over
she says, ma ma

THE FACE
AS IT MIGHT BE
OF LOVE

i touch your nose
  & what beneath

the flesh mat
thick & soft
the brain gray as goat's curd
the kind cup of your skull

when will i break this mirror of your eye

in it

the moon
drags the water
on the shadow of its back

the earth
dims
as a jewel in darkness

& my face hangs
starless
as dime-store crystal

THIS WOMAN WILL NOT BEAR CHILDREN

men might put their hands
on my belly &
feel the awful roar of seven oceans

i might fit my fullness
into them

but my mother warned me

i am not tempted
to tear the cloth
& fray those spindly nerves
tucked in tender lobes

she soothed them with her voice
crooned them to sleep
        though
i long for that electric spill
pole to pole
two vacuums sucking one light

death is my protection

kiss me on my lips
i would wake

KATHERINE DOAK

FOX SONG

He that parts us shall bring a brand from heaven,
And fire us hence like foxes.

King Lear

In birth we're fired from our hole
to grow between the howls
of scattered mates, still lusting
for the severed living and the dead.

Alone, among the spruce that stand
like jagged spearheads frozen
to the sky, the white fox barks,
"Beware, bewail, be still."

All hear his cry
and we who are the red fox kin,
conspirators who sing in packs,
reply in terrifying choir,

"Our ruddy coats are beacons to our kind;
Our song ignites the coal of night."
The calls of white and red fox mix,
the counterpoint of frost and fire.

NUNNERY

This is the nunnery

lined with withered robes
with moth holes at the back
and crosses on the front

There is no garden here

just bread, flat as cheeks
that wobble to the open and close
of the confessing mouth

There is water here

holy water, they catch it in tubs
when it rains, to sprinkle
on their wilted remains

There is no one here

but those who wait to die
none with a gleaming eye
would make the sign of crosses red on wrists

Here are the candles

they light them at night
stare long and red-eyed
and blister the thought of star-cooled skies

Here is the chair

where they cut the hair
see the curls thick on the floor
soft under bare feet

This is the door

where the young ones slip back
to see those tresses by the moon
they cry, then shift to the bell

This is the chapel

SEA OTTER,
A DREAM POEM TO MY MOTHER

Before I slept, I saw the nebula
of your ashes swirl in the sea
and smash into stars on the sand.
For hours after I hunted the shore
listening for your voice in shells
that went mute in my hand.
When I begged the sea for your face
the fog came in.

Now you surface in my sleep.
Hoarse cries sound in the bay of my ear.
You chip my eyes with rock
and lids split open like mussel shells.
I see you floating on the swell
and spill, crowned with kelp
and sleek as the sea itself
you preen and dive and glide.
I am honored beyond song.

KATHERINE DOAK

SONG OF CERES

My hands are in the garden
soil half-mooned beneath my nails
and creases laced with loam
I am Ceres
playing in my dirty mind.

All the warm days
my murmuring mouth upon the soil
with tongue I stir
the earth to moving slow
I stir the worms to a curling dance
that quivers the seed
and pounds the root
until all rushes to my touch
in green and gold;
I coax my daughters
to the sun.

Slow, then, in coming cold
my breath turns rank
with miasmal mutterings to the earth
and toxic tongue
I tear the little daughters' skirts
and leave their husks
all rustling in a row.

Sod in clumps between my teeth,
a dying misdiety,
I putter in my plot
until it sings in green with me
or cackles gray,
I pass in seasons
wait the creeping fire
to crisp both field and gardener.

CLAUDIA DOBKINS

STILL LIFE

This still life of cups mocking the table
recurs as a glint of eye,
as an ice room blown on October's window.

Your thumbs shredding plums, the skillet
where you stand, back bent, sleek as a cat.
The orange bowls gape where my laughter sticks,

the teeth edge of it slitting your voice
beating out the inevitable, each syllable
booms hollow, an echo of broken drums.

I turn, rotating on my axis of knives,
the walls ache, the lights shut,
as you tell me about her.

VOICE

It is pleasant enough here.
I have the window and the wall outside.
I have only to look down and see the rubbish,
that will keep me busy.

There's a milk container,
and a discarded mattress, look at the pee stains.
Too, on the fire escape, someone's laundry
has fallen; blue pants, a shirt, a printed scarf.

But that is not all,
there are winter trees bare as chicken bones
and animals; the wild cats chase rodents,
hang their souls on the wall.

At sunset the flood lights blink on like
individual migraines.
Across the way people draw the curtains
shutting me out.

I am looking from someone's head.
She has lent me her eyes. Should I itch
I borrow her fingers. If I pull the blinds
everything is different.

The wall recedes now, it is dark.
I listen for footsteps thinking
there is something I should do.

BRIEF EXPLANATION

What love did. The beast sleeps.
The apples sit on the window dried and waiting.
When poems yawn the air eats itself,
a good void, the shaft of my brain waits

for what you say, I am more like hunger
satiated on tubes, the beast is the curve
of a letter re-routed, it breathes in strange
winds, blinks with button eyes.

Love, say then that I have written stronger
poems; I outweigh dust, in the crumble of
earth I am a blade hating; or, let me die,
the pump of blood, the bullet of heart blasts
too deep.

If what I say rides on helium, know it can
be pricked, that the line is empty, what I
pour in the glass bell leaks, my teeth tear
blanks.

What love did. The beast sleeps.
I work to hear the sound of nothing.
The agony has gone deaf, as if each day
were the last poem I'll ever write.

CLAUDIA DOBKINS

MIRACLE WORKER

Watch me bruise the air with my hawk winged flutterings,
and the dreams I spin will fly like bee stings jabbed in
a cricket's mouth. Then the lone whine in my throat will
click like a fish bone.

I wait for your applause, applause.
In the palms of your hands, ladies and gentlemen, I see
     myself
scratching like a cat's claw, and once a month (this never
     fails)
I walk upright on a sea of blood. Let me kiss your glass
     fingers,
I can guarantee my tears plop like lava rock.

Look at me and I become visible. Only the ghost
     smooths its
hair. Watch me ooze out of myself, I will chew at my lips
with rusted tooth, like Houdini in a box, my chains rattle
their arthritic joints (there is nothing up my sleeves),

For I have been anointed with hard water.
My thighs glitter like plastic ruby jewels.
I have two mouths, both gagged. I can gurgle
like a drain both plunged and pardoned.

I wait for your applause, applause.

VIRGINIA GILBERT

BECKET

Sir Thomas Becket wore a gray sackcloth
so he would not forget the scratch of God.
Yet, not even this one hair skin and three
wool cowls, nor nocturnal prayers, penitence,
confession and absolution or his
giving the mass and solemn vespers were
enough to warm his candle-bone thin hands.
Later, when King Henry's gentlemen
crushed the pontiff's skull, they never knew
they were lighting his slender fingers.

VIRGINIA GILBERT

FOR JOHN BERRYMAN

The time came
for leaving, the shoes hardened
and the watch given
to Henry down the hall.
Once again, on the journey
to Seoul or Pittsburgh,
the Arena of Rome, the emptied seats,
arched and circular
become a part of our memory.
Wise or small,
the man of the lone eyeglass
honors the sole ticket
taker with his palm.

This, my friend, at the Gate
of departures, is the moment
of our arrival, the people
who have bought the streets,
their undershirts
worn thin, meeting you again
and you, meeting
again and again and again
the conductors of a different
language with one half
of the mustache
left on. Call it fate
or a quick tongue,
the last meanderings
of a forgotten race.
This time, forbear the taxi
or catch it on foot;
a child running by,
fallen into life,
lets his blood flow
into his hands from the pivot
of a broken skull.
This is what you asked
from the gentlest mountain
where under the squares
of pavements all our feet
rush past.

VIRGINIA GILBERT

PAX ROMANA

It will be like this.
The sky will be rubber gray,
rocks will be leveled
and birds will go underground.
Sand will crawl
across the face
of the earth and fog
will chew branches off trees.
In the early stages,
pinecones will be sold
in stores and fishing rods
will become a popular
wall decoration. The water
level will rise. Libraries
will dissemble, words will
float, become saturated,
peel off their pages,
and, the pages will be
dumb, a layer of silt
drifting to the bottom.
In the end,
there will be no source.
Water will be everywhere.

ELLEN McEVILLEY GRIFFIN

GOOD HARBOR BAY, LELAND, MICHIGAN

It's much like stopping travellers to ask directions
following landmarks all along the way
past the Koepke's vineyards by the stoney bluff,
over the road beyond the Schneider's farmhouse,
to the bend in the route that lets you know you're there.
Years later I saw the renovation they had made.
I could forgive what they had done to the terrace,
but they'd pruned the orchard to look like a Boston
    garden,
and the old chaise lounge in the living room is gone.

Far away, and though life is no longer simple,
some nights in the city I still see the moon,
and hear the authoritative roar of Lake Michigan,
over the rows of beds and sleeping children. . .
As lives go or their leaders, one might say,
that I have run into the sunset all my life,
toward a great lake, down a white sand path
with a small black dog behind me,
the elders sitting and shelling peas on the terrace.

33

RIMBAUD IN ABYSSINIA

Long ago he had walked
away the apocalypse,
the incomparable fancy
having run with the hook
all night,
and tired of the moon
and the mind
and the various organized
dreams of man.

Certainly he did not play
the prodigal son,
returning being for fools
and beggars, sympathy
not of the world
of coffee and gun-running,
only rebellion rising
each day
out of the white-winged morning
into meaning.

CONFESSION OF A YOUNG HEGELIAN

I was brought up with a myth in my mind
of the world in history, history in the world
coming to a discernible sum in time, that each
life culminates; it was later I contracted
the feeling that the best times were done.

Beyond the golden age of art and crucifixion,
learning the ending of childhood
and the old meaning of past and possible
coming to a taut conclusion:—never will
there again really be magic,
nor have you accomplished anything—

There have been times, out of time,
and real or imagined destiny
when something counted for knowing;
something before seeing the gray
steamers abandoned in the harbor,
circled by gulls, their days of hauling
coal and lumber over.

IF I ASK WHETHER THE ISLANDS

Sing whatever is well-made.

W.B. Yeats

If I ask whether the islands
   will learn from my life,
I must answer no
   surely they will learn nothing.
For the old truth
   is this: fingers of land
with no depth between
   are joined;
they publish inability
   not insularity.
I am no coward
   but I lack that greater love
that fashioned everywhere
   its violence.

There was a man—
   it would take a heron's dive
to tell his life—
   and still unfathomable
he died. Words
   will be weaker
than his beauty.
   Waters closed, the fish
was eaten, and
   the bird does not return.
Oh hills of Ireland
   if you do not miss his song
why is there everywhere
   his silence?

ELIZABETH HANSON

WALKING WITHOUT SNOWSHOES

I walk facing against the wind,
facing you, where I've been,
leaning south against the hours

Arrows of wind and icicles that
have slipped between us have now been named
They crack the dead lock on the air

We were once one skier
who was pulled apart by separate
boots. Now in opposite mounds
of snow we lick our paths clean.

Tomorrow is spring: Another crystal
ball breaks as our impatient tongues
touch tips and defrost another season

Let the goose down quilts be raised and furled
in honor of this event! Each of us will take
another corner of the heart, tug, and make a wish

ELIZABETH HANSON

DEPARTURE

Your blonde beard crushes ice into
a belly of open arms
Each strand reaches down and is held
there by wet, melted water.
The empty paintless mask is a landing field
for your smooth gliding eyes
They perch there for a quiet hour
and then slide on downward
as you rearrange your
old position scattering new
limbs and fingers over an ancient body.

You measure time in ounces of dropped sweat
and heaving onto knees and hands
fall backwards into your clothes.
Your last wish is a kiss
that you cannot feel but can only
taste the sound of. You stand there
folding a hand over every ear
and listen: It is

like the silence of a thousand fish
swimming away.

SUMMER'S DARKNESS

Leaning into the edge of the earth
(grass that has been green and folded,
brown tips and twigs)
I fumble towards your shadow
while the sun is still quite red and low.
I am grasping onto the darkness,
something that *is* there,
in your arm, in your face, in your back I cannot see,
while you touch me lightly and force
without strength that greenness out of my eye.
The sky in your eyes sends signals
and I know where you really are—
Slithering under me into browner ground, more fertile.
I speak into cracked ears, partially
gone deaf, "I'll swing over that crevice
with you; give me another push."

Now I am on my knees, crawling, falling
into the edge of the earth.
The sky does not follow me down here,
but some strange light follows you
over to the other side, and I see
that you, at least, have made the leap.

There is a blue and red tent pitched on the
other side, sleeping two, in another
forest gone greener. The trees, the sun
aren't as red or sagging and you can
no longer face downward to where
the earth split apart. I stay
alone here only because there is
no light, no dark; just a maze
of edges that I float through now
and then, just to pass the time.

PATRICIA HENLEY

NEAR CALEDONIA

Leaves bed the woods,
cottonfields rust in disuse.
US Highway 301 guts the eastern seaboard,
throat to groin, bank after national bank.
A smoked lilac sky prevails. Grease
clings from holiday barbecues,
the homes and pool halls,
gray on gray. Deeper on
in Virginia, a worn barn kneels
into the earth.

Near Caledonia, catch a fleeting glimpse,
a fat black woman, her hip nudging
the screen door ajar,
she wears a red fedora,
her blouse splashes wide flowers,
her skirt creases beneath her broad belly.
She sings to the deaf winter.

RETURNING FROM THE FUNERAL

Driving east,
the mountain range lies ahead,
a pale blue bone. Clouds scuttle
like putty crabs. I am anxious to be there,
away from the aging, the smothering talk
of the past. In death, they cleaned you,
drew your trembling lips together,
placed the pearl rosary just so
in your still hands I never knew
but shaking from the palsy's sting.

I inherit a pasteboard box
of documents and love letters,
proving you a passionate woman.
My lover quotes the *Tibetan Book of the Dead:*
there should be no mourning
and there isn't. I want to know
I'm alive, eating egg rolls and making
love all night long, tinging
the death with my blood pealing
like church bells, leaving
the flat land, the farmhouses
of my youth, all set
in such staid symmetry.

PATRICIA HENLEY

DAYS OF RE-ENTRY

I

Evening cracks:
a lime peeling wraps
the muddy mushrooming clouds.
In the car, we each occupy
our own durable shadow
waiting for that laggard,
compassion, to catch us up.
The hilly horizon expands
and contracts, squeezing us
out the funnel's end of Christmas
two days past.

II

An unexpected thaw
floods the valley near Mt. Savage.
Snow rests in torn pages
on the land. Rust laces tin roofs.
We drink fruit brandy. Amid family
hugging and baking and quarreling,
we rescue one another, inching,
inching, serious as firemen
and just as breathless, wild-eyed.
Sunset blinds the suburban windows,
dusts the scrub hills pink.

III

In the city,
the train station ceiling
is pockmarked by design,
chilled marble. Waiting
for the southbound, we are quiet,
ransomed. We grow like grafted plants,
burning without ashes in the fire
of the gauze blond sun.

TIME OUT

Nobody told her it was time to go.
She signed herself in
at Perry Point Veteran's Hospital
with all the other crazy ladies,
ex-wacs and waves, playing gin rummy
and waiting for cigarette privileges.

Once she posed, arrogant,
her curly head thrown back,
on the fender of a Model-T Ford
painted Towncar Cream. At seventeen,
she forged her age, enlisting,
using her father's trade in the motorpool,
knowing like the alphabet, one wrench
from another. Here is a woman
who wore no bra in 1945, the first woman
to ride in the nose of a B-52.

Once there were new things to do
and nobody named Lucille
in a wrinkled hospital gown playing
ragtime all day long on the ward piano.
After each time, she returned
trembling and hopeful,
her fingernails painted fire-engine red.

ELAINE H. JENNINGS

each night

each night
just before dusk
men pregnant with retirement
men pulled under sleeveless undershirts
walk their square spotted dogs
dogs which are not made anymore

peeking eye-circled dogs
bred on table waste & hair-streaked laps
of women gone to their graves
gone also on this walk at dusk
like low slung foreign voices
each foot doubting the other

closing this speck
between alley fences
under the hood of wires
walking, walking to death

i am riding a lion. . .

i am riding a lion
to the library

he will park himself
at each corner of its mouth
and remain the same thing
            from which he came

i go inside, way inside,
and make love with the books

the lion waits,
his beautiful gray paws
being a quarter after something,
wanting to be a quarter before

a bell fastens its sense
on time
the library closes,
listening into here, into
the way back sounds

a flight of words releases
itself over the fountain;
i check out no books
they have read me

ELAINE H. JENNINGS

WEATHER REPORT

After the glass shower
we slept like flowers
at night, folded into
the grass, un-electric
little thinky grubs
fat on the day's brainwad,

chilling overnight
like jello, fatigued
with pushing secrets
(to life yes of course)
at the herds of gray folk

drinking and smoking and
screwing for it
in the dark
with each other.

THERE IS NO TIME

when we finally
do reach our lives
when we finally
get to the parts
that say

yes, we are us
there is no more

we talk at them
with sore throats
we rent crude spaces
to them
so much we rent
that there is often nothing
to write about
after all that talking/feeling

as years race by
storing the little hopes
of dust in our hands
we talk at our fingers
they are proof
that we feel

      water
      sex
      a child's hair
      morning as it feels
             early

then suddenly by trick
or folly (never accident)
it is next time
and we cannot retrieve
though backwards we go

we steal it
with adolescent fingers,
a hubcap to roll
into tomorrow

KAREN L. KENT

C44

womens ward
stacked up
down the middle
around both sides
enema douche cunt shave demeral
shots in leg
cunt cancer   cobalt
radium implants   weekends
out of the ward
back on mondays
for more cure

three day
patients having babies
& sterilizations
leave this home
of their mostly older
sisters   mothers
three days
a long time   have
a longer time   after leaving

belly slit
navel slit
bandaid sterilization
& scrape the womb blood
belly fill   w 4 liters   carbon
dioxide   tipped on head
table does it
aftermath   general
operation   recovery   waddle
around a few days

get a new love
get a new apartment
going to raise
plants & jungle
grass   throw
a few clay pots
& fits   im scared
seems   too   easy
what happens   after
when one is no longer one
one moves on

KAREN L. KENT

white sheer tieback curtains . . .

white sheer tieback curtains
three upstairs bedroom windows
my windows
my grandmothers old house
with bedrooms like this
green ferns ivies grape leaves
next door wild raspberries ripe
my aunt used to make
beautiful piano music
now i listen
to eric satie piano
remembering first
practice scales
smell of new
days lazy days
watching white cat cross
street lick & clean
no backache stiff muscles
or sore head
feels like thirty years ago
blue willow china plates
rhubarb pudding cake
& grandmas house before moving
to town
farm home brick front steps
dark underexposed print
of dining & living rooms
scratchy blue sofa
wood stove in kitchen plants in window
bright sun & playing outdoors
or in the barn helping grandpa
with chores
always listening to   &   love
still coming
to me   a small girl   lying on
bed   by window   living
with cancer

dead grandpa & grandma & aunt
no   window
screen   keeping me   away

mother your children give you . . .

mother   your children give you
grief & grandchildren   i would

take you to california if i
could give you glamour   put

fathers life of labor into
travel instead   snow is

falling now, after last nights
rain, covering the branches

glittering cold   pure   hard
to crack like your solid head

of norwegian stubborness
working time to death   seeing

sun green & grapes   the sea
always inside   there are

always excuses for not finding
the right time   the blood rises

& falls   our bodies still are
sturdy   the fields are dormant

tombed in snow   winter
animals sleep   a dark blotch

of a calf   too young to be
born lies frozen

the icy chatter of birds
fills the air   the sounds

of many heavy wings beating
and we are gone

Alan walks with his head . . .

Alan walks with his head
upside down

says hes looking
for those wings
he lost
when he was born

he drew a picture
of how he looks
when he lives
in another world

he likes to go
back every now & then

stops in
at his office
to visit
his grandma   whos resting
there   now that
shes   stopped
living   on earth

brings her
his favorite cookies

he watches cowboys fishing
roping the fish   catch
them by their   hair

leans over   his table
to see the ocean   picks
up a drop of water to
swim in

when hes tired/hungry
he   eats up
the   universe

GLORIA BUSSEL KOSTER

INTERPRETATION
for cecile winters

I am filled with fire oaths and utterances.
Somehow,
they come out like peaceful blue beads.
A clear March sky thinks she'll get me for a companion.

My friends are awed by my amazing rocking,
breeze-like
as though I'd adjusted the world
to let me wander safely in its cavities.

Memory
a mother, in some grade-school story, kept wiping her
        hands, her losses,
her aproned form upright in the doorway.
She is my model,
my intangible, fictional self.

Oh God, I address you as a giant vocabulary word.
Perhaps it is freedom you wanted to give me.
In 1972, I can wear a plumed hat or a devilish black dress
        to the store.
For the patterns have lifted in my case,
I am a precedent.

GLORIA BUSSEL KOSTER

EARLY MORNING SONG: THE SNOWSTORM

Fogless morning but black
snowing and biting back
at my rough hands, frozen key.
Falling into a light box with wheels,
I join the caravan of non-color.
I enter my car in the assembly line of ice.

The steering wheel grips, and God
skates on his favorite acre.
Oh my sled has privacy, will never be
revived or pushed by the medics on this white, white
    floor.

And today there is no red or green or yellow.
The intersection gets by with her muted dentist's light
that winks like the moon at traffic.
And my whole body blanches
to glide by on such uncertain terms.

Children come and go like clear bottles in the road.
They look so slow and eerie.
Yet I, who have craved such transparency,
sing songs for daytime and songs with WABC
and wait for yesterday's world to snap back.

THE DINER

Spooning in gravy,
you were sustained by reverie.
In the diner with its chrome and mirrors,
you had only yourself
to touch like cool water.

Five miles back
the grocer's son had stood statuesque
over tomatoes and yellow ripples of squash.
You had wanted to take the boy
into the woods and cover him with flowers,
steal his Indian couplet name,
and claim his space at the table of pots and aromas.

In childhood you would have done just that.
New forms had come simply to your small body,
the trees and the people in town waiting to enter;
their salvation was
your play transformation.
But the grocer's boy, a confusion of red lips and
        separateness,
only waved you off to the highway, to here.
Coming up the road, you saw the conifers
bow out of your way,
their thinning tops, their thousand flat needles
trilling.

Propped in the booth,
you sat behind place mats and glasses.
But loneliness took your solidity,
took your gray-haired mass
like spilled and spreading water.

MARILYN KRYSL

DREAMS FROM WAR

Men, bloody, approach the house
from the trees. One, two, strayed
from the war, they have been wandering
the forest, looking for their death.
In the deaths of so many
others their own death eludes them.

Earlier some grass beside a stream
seemed like a woman's hair. *Hush, hush,*
like skirts, the branches of firs. What this
reminds **them of** these men do not now
remember. The kisses of women have dried,
flaked from their lips. Isn't that a
fox on the path, glimpsed through snow?

Maybe the house is asleep. It is white,
steam on the panes. Something ordinary, a broom
left by the step, the owner abroad. On the table
part of a loaf. Now the men are dizzy.

In a half loaf of bread a man can sleep
without regrets. Wet flakes, whirling
softly, bits of white cake. In the woods
they gnawed the inner bark of saplings.

Their weariness is pure,
like snow. By it they intend
nothing. But maybe the house is a trap.
Is a pie cooling on the sill?

Far to the south children sleep in the beds
with their mothers. The women stroke the children
like little cats. Fuzz gathers on the floor.
Hibiscus float in glass bowls. The women doze
endlessly. Yards are lush, untrimmed,
empty. The hum of the gas heater
steady. The women's dreams are gray,

old pillows ripped open.
In the tissue paper stories they read to the children
bears wear suits and silk hose.

SUMMER SOLSTICE

In the barn stallions stand
and sleep. Their pause is
huge—immense bells no one
is tolling. The dog whines
in his trance and goes on
dreaming under Jupiter

and I sink down, seared by
moonlight, into the cavernous
dark. The grass is cool as
silk, and the smell of earth
is the sweet, milky
stench of the cradle.

I rest between the first and final thoughts.

MARILYN KRYSL

LECTURE WITH SLIDES, FILM CLIPS AND TAPE

Soft morning.   Sycamores.   In this one some women pass,
sharp, like crows.   Pecking.   Going
shopping. Notice that the street
is a magazine—bulldozer, jackhammer and crane
a fashionable backdrop. Now, in the film
notice the stiffness in torso
and neck. Reminiscent of straightjackets. Here
suicide is a luxury. (A breeze and the promise of the air
did not take on film.)

These women believe, except for
small doubts. Small doubts
without pattern, at irregular intervals,
like spotting. Seeing a physician
is a way of waiting out dreams.
On your left the inner office
of a specialist—simple as a chalice.
And the outer office—a closeup—
knitting needles clicking like a set of teeth.
Notice the number of appointments
leading to other appointments
and afterward the woman buys the perfect
dress. A cross section, the garment
like a way of life—terrace, white iron table
with nothing on it that must be eaten
or drunk or read or condemned or fondled.
A dress that is a place where she can
sleep. But they can't

sleep. Though the night is smooth, the sky
studded with galaxies, and we heard
sharp cries floating on the air like ash—
but the sound ceased abruptly, as though
taped. Night after night
we filmed each one pacing the parquet,
smoking by fits and starts in the dark.
Apparently the small but genuine perfection of grass
holds no joy, the classic peace of sprinklers whirring
cannot sooth them. Instead—focus—
the brain's one central, pulsing, compound eye
smolders. And in this slide a woman at midnight

drinks a glass of water. See how she admires
the ice cubes' easy numbness
but on film watch the ice cubes
cloud, little rectangles
of salt. Driven by terrible
thirst she quits the house to wander

here—the city's core—that sleeplessness that corresponds
to her own.
                    But we have said nothing
about the man. You have noticed
how little evidence we have, how seldom they are
present. Those few we observed
remained in the cabs of the municipality's
earth-moving machines,
and on the center screen
in the fullblown perfume of the sun
only the iron sculpture

of a president, riding to the first and only and unceasing
war. (Is he already
dead on his horse?) Now

the tape. You will hear
their blood sobbing
for our lost gentleness.

DIANE LEVENBERG

ALCHEMY

Friday afternoon: chicken eggs
soaking on the drainboard (for soup)
My mother in our sunny pantry
grinding liver   wiping perspiration
with her apron   brief Yiddish
phrases in hurried phone conversations

DIANE LEVENBERG

Six years of watching these
before-the-Sabbath preparations
nourishing me through the next nineteen
(A Jewish mother's suicide:
It's all right   there's a box of farina
in the cupboard
and a jar of chicken soup
in the Frigidaire)

Twenty years later
the same smell of onions
I had almost forgotten the magic
of *gribinis** in rendered chicken fat
hard boiled eggs   chicken livers
and a Jewish mother to transform them

You remind me
(suddenly a six-year old again)
it's the wrong day (Sunday)
the liver hasn't been salted
and while my mother
took frequent sips of phone conversation
you are drinking whiskey and water

Yet   this feminine alchemy—you
feeding me golden onions from your fingers
as I gratefully watch the rest
become my private eucharist

I remind you that
my mother knew I would watch you
prepare this tasty dish
taste of it
and feel loved and whole again

*gribinis: Yiddish for crisply fried onions.

61

DIANE LEVENBERG

DREAMING OF CONN-EDA

> The moral of the *Story of Conn-eda* is: follow
> your unconscious intuitive forces blindly and
> with confident faith. They will carry you
> through your perilous trials. Cherish them; be-
> lieve in them; do not frustrate them with intellec-
> tual distrust and criticism; but permit them to
> move and sustain you.
>
> Heinrich Zimmer
> *The King and the Corpse*

Conn-Eda hid himself in horse's hide
thus warding off the dangers beyond the gate
It was easier in pagan legends
We have God   the death of God
ritual and life with no ritual
less innocence and more evil
What covers us is our own flesh
and less than gates hold back the danger

I am thinking of removing coverings
of tearing wide the curtain
gauze netting   cheesecloth mesh
a flimsy thing in which the knots get tighter
I am thinking of embracing my darkness
There is danger here
other levels   other depths

Here in my marriage bed
I am covered by a quilt
sewn with sinews I have discarded
made of skins I have flayed
throughout these years of revelation

I am thinking of Conn-Eda
I am dreaming of Conn-Eda
I am thinking of removing coverings
One has been shielding a seductive light
The other has been kept in the sun too long

There is a nighttime draft I can feel
through the places where the skins have cracked
Conn-Eda kisses me good-night
My husband sighs in his sleep
and wraps his leg around me
I am dreaming of Conn-Eda

OUT OF THE DESERT

All that time wasted
wandering the Sinai of
my false idea
thinking I had to bring you
the magic of manna the
ingenuity of those wonderful cakes
(nourishing but tasteless)

And like the whore of Givah
twelve vital parts of her
distributed tribe by tribe
I thought that's how
you'd take me
Would you be Judah
and ask for the head
Or Reuben and ask
for the heart
Or Levi who took
nothing but knew
how to divide

Having no magic
means of survival
I bring you
this naked woman
having led herself
out of the desert

DIANE LEVENBERG

AFTER SELECTING THE WEDDING INVITATIONS

Last night
after selecting the wedding invitations
(the Hebrew lettering seemed fitting
signs of a Quamran Mystic
but David Empire Royal
goes better with Park Avenue)
we went looking for a poem
to celebrate
our printed commitment

Feast of Saint Gennaro
melange of variegated pork
and petty profiteering
Carnival crowds pushing through
the streets reflected in
shallow pools of sewaged olive oil

An aging couple
dancing on the sidewalk
Italian tarentella
I saw horas
and kazatzkas
my wedding
wondering
will we be this happy
dancing freely openly
a poem after all
the added edited stanzas of life

Last night I dreamed
a cat with ivory claws
attacked me

MARY LOGUE

SOUTH WIND

I am leaving
My clothes take flight
Their wings full of the wind

In the night
When the ghosts sit in the living room
I will light a candle
Walk down the stairs
Out the back door

The children
I see their cheeks
Pale moons filling the night

The sun is up
I am gone
I'm walking down highway 35
The wind is from the south.

INDIAN WARRIOR

I will draw you
With lines that are dark
Your face is dark
A black plain with little brush
I will draw you alone
I will not draw you
With your wife
She is your gentle side
She has fallen from the wings of a bird.

WINTER POND

The muskrats
Swim in the pond
Tunneling in the ice

The ice froze
It caught the reflection of trees,
Stalks of white and withered leaves,
The muskrats are busy
Releasing them.

The last white duck
Struggles on the pond
As she watches
The water crystallize around her
She strokes with webbed feet
Clears a liquid hole.

The glass pond
A fallen mirror
I lay on my belly
Let my nose freeze to the surface.

KATHLEEN LUBECK

From *SONS*

Through the noonday sun
I can see our oldest, James,
Walking up the road to his father.
James, the renegade, who
Left one night with stormy looks.
Bequeathing me an empty place at the table,
James, who returned from
Two weeks of working as a ranchhand;
James, lost from our farm,
Who found his father.
James, who cried at his father's proffered hand,
Who smiled when his father said calmly,
"Families do not need pruning, son."

(more)

Then I see Damian walking towards town,
Down the dusty road,
Breathing in only the sky and fields and sun,
Which he would transform into words.
Damian with his library books,
Damian with his eyes for beauty,
Damian with his gift of translating into words.
He would work with the Idaho fields, yes;
And then write
Words flowing with
Life.

Adam was the boys' boy,
Catching black Tanya,
The wildest horse,
And riding her out where
The meadows rose up
Into mountains.
Adam who chased after deer.
Adam who flew with the wind.
Adam who was thrown, and
We thought dead,
Till his father prayed for him.
Adam who smiled from the pillows
As Michael read to him after work.
Adam who walked and rode again,
Through his father's covenant with God.

TERESA A. McCARTHY

MISERICORDIA

Mother, I have loved you long
And long even after they
locked the grate and carried out
the Paschal Lamb.
You are always the same, sad dream
with whom I have slept these many years;
Guadalupe, brown and smiling
Welcomes me home again. . .
Toledo's patriarchs glide by on
Vanishing tapers of sable stoles,
Shaking sharp fingers of ice,
White-hot and accusing,
Burning through stained glass,
They have melted me away.

TERESA A. McCARTHY

ANITA, LA MALDITA

Anita, Lady of most whole silence,
Lady of kinetic Cocaine
comes by nodding at my door;
When she dances, she is my body,
and the brackish maelstrom
of her owl eye
flows into the hollow crevice
of my dream.

She nurses me with the rich
green milk of cobras
and she wraps me in the
dark red light of her pointed tongue.

Anita, Lady of broken treaties,
leers at the Man of perfect
understanding
who plans to drive between us
his wedge of bone-hard logical steel.

When he threatens with his
penknife,
Anita, Lady of lost cauldrons,
will conjure a whirlwind
from her white robe to save us,
to fly us back under the
dark loving mangroves of our blood.

TERESA A. McCARTHY

VISIT PERU:
OF STONED INCAS' LAND

Sacsahuamán, you know, where they drag out
all those spitting llamas for the cameras;
When they milk them, tiny drops of cocaine
form all wrapped in sanitary, plastic bags.
You see, señor, our ancestors used no mortar
for these walls, yet solid just like this
they stand five thousand years.
The girl from Frankfurt wears small halters;
Her back's a garden of pimples, just under
my nose where she is still trying to speak French.
God, haven't you guessed why it was there
Man first ate weiners?
They tell us now some freak from Saturn
Built these cities, landed here in 1325;
Not here, stupid, but Nazca near the coast.
A Spaniard first discovered this plan to
Crush all talk these spaced-out heads
Inherit brains of gold.

NANCY MAIRS

WINTER MORNINGS

I think of all the women behind locked doors
of small houses, each sealed in her inviolate space:
dust-free, measured by carpeting and draperies.

They watch their husbands and their children
from a safe distance. They breathe as little
as possible. They rarely shout. They shiver a lot,
in spite of heavy sweaters, because their bones
are cold. They consider growing old; age never comes.

They stand so still: their straight mouths
framed by bitten lips; their hearts contracted
to the weight and sheen of polished alabaster;
their palms marked by the bitter sign of the red
half-moon. Their eyes are empty as sucked eggs.

I watch them, line on line, like clothes
strung out in winter. And when I have looked
so long that frost needles the backs of my eyes,
then I go home, and close and lock the door.

WAKING TO LEOPARDS

With my eyelids still squeezed
I push my face
through the tangle of dry blades
into the crumbling clots
of dirt at the roots
and listen for the leopards
lurking in the tall grass.
They stir and the grass
like silk hisses
against their bodies. I smell
the heat from their black fur.
The roar of their purring
pours over me like heavy surf:
My flesh weakens with the weight.
When I lift my head their eyes
are polished and yellow
sunlight through amber.
Their rough tongues lick my skin
until it dissolves into honey
and heat. I push my fingers
through their fur to the tensed
tough sinews beneath the skin.
I cling there, and wait.

NANCY MAIRS

POISON

She remembers seasons
when her blood in the heat
bubbled until she shook.
Now she sees it thin and tepid,
the stream from an old spigot
faintly red with rust.

Her vagina shrivels and twists
like a shrunken sleeve.
And her heart, that was
fat and red and hot as the palm
of a midsummer poppy,
contracts to a small red fist
beating against the bars,
the white bone,
the white teeth in the grin
of imprisonment.

She has grown small,
mean as a pit viper,
venomous and quick. Her bones
rattle a warning, her breath
hisses along her tongue.
No one would dare
kiss her quiet smile.

THE DEPARTURE OF THE WOMEN

The men trample the earth.
Beneath their huge feet the dust
puffs in swollen balls
that burst on their chests.
Their hands swing slow arcs
against the brown air. Under the old
sun their furred torsos are
red boles in the hot wind.
Their penises, strangled serpents,
slap their thighs right
left. Their buttocks clench.

Where are the women?
Have they gone to the well?
Have they gone to the war?
They are hidden
like water. They have become
the blue fluid that oozes
from under rocks and lies
beside them dark and quiet.
They have become the other
rocks. Tired, powerful,
they are seeping
back into the earth alone.

POLLY MANN

SMILE AT THE BIRDIE

Dimpling in his cheeks
An M-16 rifle
Making him seem a pygmy—
Nine-year-old Ser Tao,
Defender of
Site 32, Bouam Long,
North of the Plain of Jars.

MUSEUM ITEM 237

In a square case
To the left of the Oneida arrowheads,
To the right of the uniforms of five wars,
Across from a miniature replica of a wood cookstove,
You recline—tilted—on velvet—
Enclosed in a gold-framed shadowbox,
You—phantasmagoric wreath of human hair
From the Picketts and Strongs of Lyon County,
Plucked or constructed in eighteen fifty-one.

Were you willed from father to son?
Did you rest for years in some airless attic?
Were you one of many held in housewives' laps
Created by lamplight in long wintry nights?

Who made you, wreath?
It must have been "she."
What "he" would spend hours
Making hair into spidery flowerets?

What care—what concentration—
"This is your hair, Maude,
See how pretty it makes up.
That dark stuff is Dad's beard,
And the blonde rosette was from Ann at four."

Hair wreath you are—but what?
Hair wreath.

POLLY MANN

ATLAS' DAUGHTER

Twenty-four kilometers to the camp
Where we homeless ones will be
Provided the refuge of
Wire that bites.
The little ones muted by fear
Walk silently,
An occasional tear
For our gentle old water buffalo—Pham Ngo
Who expired in the great smoke cloud
Of our hut and rice field.

On my back—a weight equal almost to my own.
It might have been a stone but it moves restlessly.
The sun rises and sets in each kilometer.
We rest often.
Finally I unburden my back of the pack—
My twelfth-year husband who
Had he legs
Would weigh far more.

ADRIANNE MARCUS

LINES FOUND ON AN ENVELOPE
Once I said, always. *Once, God knows, is enough to*
  establish relevance.

On the front of the envelope,
my own handwriting; a message
to me. There's no name, nor,
I suppose, any need for one.
I know who it's for, and like
cliches, or axioms,
it applies.

I think of you, momentarily,
letters I won't write,
the face that returns in
dreams to confront me
when I am most speechless;
the savage regret
of waking. Even together,
we have nothing to say.

(more)

ADRIANNE MARCUS

The telephone becomes
my enemy, connects numbers
I can't forget
and the insistent ringing.

This silence is what I'm
learning. Always.
There is enough relevance
without me. I bear
the weight of the
year like an unwanted
birthday; candles I can't
blow out, the breath
trying to extinguish itself,
over and over.

Is this what forever means?
March arrives, still storming
with February,
the wind toppling the light
rooted plants, the blossoms
torn from the branch.
The whole house shudders
pleated with wind
and flaring rain.

I dream of ships
to ride out the weather;
ornate rooms of dark
mahogany, heavy furniture
and persian rugs.
What is solid lasts
longer than the reeling
wind, the sharp call,
or the phone
that I finally answer
to find the line
gone dead
in the storm.

LETTERS, RETURNED

You send them back to me. I
will write no more. Your face dissolves
like salt in water, the slow reprisal
banished from the dream.
This is no simple exorcism,
changing love to distance.

The brilliant flowers of the night,
Magnolias, hold their ivory petals
fastened to the moon, the bruised
indifferent moon. I walk outside
into the flesh-like air, holding
my letters. Only an owl,
my own voice, performs a litany
of Who. Question and answer.

Taking a match, I burn.
The old words flare, become
paper, ash, nothing
to remember. In the bright darkness
the last light fixes a new moon,
a quartered smile, that curves
like a sickle in the black sky,
sharp as promises.

ADRIANNE MARCUS

BEYOND LOGIC

For weeks I thought of you,
then, less and less. Spirit
and Flesh. How eagerly the
two combine and then must
separate, return to familiar
places, names that hang
securely on the tongue.

The light behind the mirror.
The unimaginable design.
What small rockets of the
mind explode like planets,
binary, and nova, burn
beyond the night to show
us all the places
where the heart
has precedence?

Whatever name convicts us,
holding out the letters
of the year and calls
us mad, or foolish, or
diseased, it is no curse
to love. I have saved
no one, and will not hesitate
to take your hand in mine,
your body as it is,
and burn together.

Time, distance,
defy all logic
until we falter
in the first sin:
Reason.

ADRIANNE MARCUS

THE BOOK ENDS, IMMORTALITY BEGINS.

When the book is closed, the
characters fall into mute
sleep. What remains is
celebration. The best

become us, having eaten
in our company, enjoyed our bodies
in the fierce hour of love. We
are kind to each other, because

of them, permit them faces
that never age. They
are the first gods we are given,
and suffer, inadequately,

our interpretations. Someone
has dreamed them pure. Bring
offerings, healing sprigs
of rosemary, chamomile flowers

to ease their passage, wordless,
into myth. Be kind. Fathers
and lovers bear no children
perfect as these.

MARY MOORE

IN THE CABIN OF LOST FIR SMELLS

i

In the cabin of lost fir smells,
Resinous
From the severed pad
Of quills,

We ate auspicious fish
For luck
And walked out
Under the concupiscent moon.

ii

We lie all night
By that half-fire
Of chilled pinecones,
You drifting off

Into your future
As rivers will go on
Through awkward hills
Bearing flotilla of bones
Furs, skins,
Like afterbirths and ruins
Of what you were.

Hollows, culverts, ravines:
My body, singed
With absence,
Smoked like river-stones
At dawn.

iii

In the cabin of lost fir scents,
Which became the scent
Of all loss,

I smelled
That hair-fine mist
The ten thousand things
Give off
Into the sun

That smell of river-stones
And departure.

LI PO

My mother-in-law hates
Alcohol
And never heard
Of Li Po,
Sailing his last poems
In paper boats
Across the moon, the mountain
The lake

SEEDING

Hulling peas,
She savors her
Previous lives,

Remembering
How she danced
With the trollop muse.

Recalling fruition
In a blue plum.

Once she was a witch
Of seed pods
And omens,
Doors and portents
A student of beginnings.
Now the past
Is fat in her
Lolls on her tongue
Like an orange
A finely felt,
Formal fruit

Reduced
Sucked clean of juice
But not quite gone
To seed.

THE SALESMAN

Smelling coffee
And waiting for bread to rise,
Things pluck at my mind
Like the beaks of birds

And the door-to-door salesman
Knocks, bringing the afternoon
Of plum blossoms
And I buy whatever he sells
Follow him home
To his evening bath
To clear water receding down
The thigh
Steam rippling the room
Clear water on the edge of flesh

He sells the open door
The spoken yes
And ignorant
Recedes into his own
Animal door.

I hum in the kitchen.
At the window, a bud protrudes
From its pubic husk.
The wind comes up at eleven.
I water the rain fern.

ROSALIE MOORE

LETTER TO BELDEN

In St. Louis as at Fountainbleau there is
A park too large to walk in
Where welcome becomes a handicap.
The police on guard,
A patch on each heart like a trump:
They smile, I walk,
I wear myself out saying thankyou.

And you, no thanks to you,
Belden my enemy—
You married my daughter
You shifter of weights and loves.
Now among peacocks and apes
        I wander,
Expecting wonders, deserving
        homage.

The zoo gives none,
Not the pelican's loose beak
And unhindered eye.
An alligator's beveled mass slides off
Like a discarded purse.

The cabarets that worked so well by gaslight
Do not delight me now:
Nudge of the searchlights,
Bulb after flaring bulb,
And each one telling
That I am this horrible light show.

Or markets in passing,
The meat in the showcases elderly;
The raw dead Sundays;
The ghettos of grieving windows.
And those, with their chattel,
Whose faces are watching like lanterns.

And you, no thanks to you, Belden
        my enemy:
You—dispossessing the poor, in
        the heat of the day—
Wrenching the white refrigerators
        hoarsely
Onto the moveable dollies.

           (more)

The blacks are moving, and
The clairvoyant stain:
They are pulling their shadows out
Like the wings of doves.

It is more than absence,
More than abandonment,
More than love gone elsewhere.
It comes up under the sidewalks
And shatters the city.
The shutters are drawn,
But the air is still strong as a carnival.

We serve what we understand,
But what we fail to,
We love like a passionate answer.

In the town where the traffic
Is turning itself to jazz,
And the jays take off from the sound
Like devisive brooms,
Is a statue of Louis,
The patron saint of this city.

Pass without notice,
Missourians, eaters of lard.

Perhaps the Missouri I despise
Has its cardinal uses,
And the King, who was never here,
Has nothing to say.

RUBEE DREHER MOXLEY

SATURDAY NIGHT

Yellow platform shoes, purple bell-bottoms, orange silk
 shirt—
Saturday Night.
M.D. double 20 wine, strawberry Boone's Farm, four no
 trump—
Man, let's get it on.
Digging Aretha's beat, freaking out on Issac Hayes—
Saturday Night.
Barbecue ribs, fried chicken—what a greasing.
Shuckin and jivin on the block, tracking the cute foxes,
 hunting your mainstuff—
Saturday Night.
Rolling snake's eyes, turning on your Dr. Feelgood, and
 not feeling any pain.

RUBEE DREHER MOXLEY

OL' TIM LEGION

Come dear sisters and brothers
while you is clothed in your right mind
call Jesus, his line ain't never busy.
Sinner man crawl out of drinking dens.
De master give us milk and honey.
Sister play soft music—cause I
wants soft money.

Repent:
Fall on your knees chullin—repent you
whore mongers—back sliders—gamblers.
Tho yo sins be red as crimson—God will
make them white as snow.
Git on the train of salvation—Jesus is de
engineer.
Git on de train of salvation—it ain't never late.
Git your one-way ticket to heaven
They is waitin at the Pearly Gates.
Now, let's pass the collection plate.

6TH AND WALNUT STREET

I remember zoot-suited pimps
with conked hair who kept stables
of beige women in shotgun houses
that needed face lifts at 6th and
Walnut Streets.

Where rat-infested movie houses sold
day old popcorn that smelled
of rancid butter

When Bucheart's had white buffalo
sandwiches for 15¢ and
Teenage boys sported black eyes and
bruised chins, a sign of manhood.

While jackleg preachers peddled cheap
grace from flatbed trucks and
sad eye hookers dressed in high fashioned
wigs and fishnet stockings prayed for
one more trick.

CAROLE OLES

POEM FOR MY HANDS

O scapegoats! How you grew chaste
under the ruler. Knuckles rose up
like onions. O sourdough palms,
you fermented in the captivity
of fingers folded on schooldesks.

Thumbs, worry beads I never misplace,
you are the rudders of civilization.
Pointers, you taught me to read;
held the words down on the page.
First comers, tall men, you sing
the low note in the penmanship trio.
Ring fingers, you extras, must study
to love yourselves nude. Pinkies,
little pickers and diggers,
. . .my last, favorite children.

O hands, you bridges; apostles:
when the hooded one pulls up
in his convertible, singing me his
you're the lover I have waited for

when he presses you to the cold
space of his lips, escorts you
past well-wishers to the place
of hingeless doors,

then you will be amnesiacs.
Forgetting sun and dishes, corduroy
and apricots. Forgetting buckles,
envelopes and safety pins.
Forgetting my love's beard,
that stiff penalty of touch.
Remembering only the long ribbon
you always knew
you would have to follow back.

CIRCLING

The yellowjacket breaks its throat
with alarms. I wake, having watched
a woman's balcony crumble under her
without a sound. The yellowjacket
bounces between two sheets of glass.
By tonight it will relax.

The child is coming towards me,
something in her doll carriage.
I see it is a rabbit.
It was hiding under our flowers.
The eyes were open.
I make her scrub it off her hands.

By 8 P.M. a mirror breaks.
The angel turning on a music box
shatters by half-past.
I lock the doors and draw
the children close.
I sing a moat around them
against what circles just outside.

THE PRICE OF BREAST IN LAS VEGAS

In the bars, the gambling rooms
all the best nightspots
silicone breasts cantilever
the drink trays; breasts
ride the footlights;
breasts are the trophy
over the doorway.
Breasts is the password.

So when he promises
breast augmentation
the girls leap.
Three-inch needles sink in.
His nostrils never quiver
as he pumps Johnson's Wax,
bootspray at sixty dollars a shot.
Going in, it looks like rich milk
tricked back. Coming out
is another story.
There is no small print
to tell of the pain.

One woman's breasts
five years later grow golfballs,
meteors burning holes
in her sleep.
Another wakes from radical
surgery with nipples pinned
under her arms.
Some permanently drop
from the chorus line,
silicone olive oil
oozing into their brains.

The survivors shower alone now.
They turn from the children.
Nightly they put out
on librium rafts
beyond the ruined orchards.

BROTHER AT ONE WEEK

Brother's cradle
doesn't rock
to lullabies
Mother doesn't hum.

So perfect in the box,
he is too perfect.
Maiden aunts
dab monogrammed hankies:
it's all for the best.

Mother's sails
hang slack
in the calm,
her smile capsizes.
Seaweed
and sandy blue beds
are on her mind.

Tomorrow Mother
will curl her hands
into trowels.
She will rake the earth
with her teeth
to carve out a hole,
a quite small burrow.
Tucking him in,
with mother-gut
she will sew up
the gash.

GERRYE PAYNE

For three days. . .

For three days
I've wanted to get married.
It came on suddenly, like a summer
thunderstorm in west Texas,
a nightmare, or
violins.

I wear a long white
Mexican skirt,
half-hysterical virgin
waiting for the ceremony.

I bring flowers into the house.

I am the last bride in the world, the only one left.
I circle the sun and moon
in my canoe full of hope,
cultivating the wind.

CLARITAS

The light, glinting off the bracelet,
described her arm, surrounded her
with emptiness, and the need came
to break up the aura,
with some hard flashes, thick colors,
impasto laid on with a knife;
or perhaps with a roll
in a muddy field where the grasses
and the seeds of grasses
would stick to her arms, would leave there
traces as patterns without cause,
as paths through which
we all might go.

There was a time. . .

There was a time when we all were dancers
in bark skirts, protected by warriors,
with stars illuminating our breasts.

Now I spend an afternoon
scraping paint off the door
down to the wood,
inventing the moon, the waterfall, the sky.

The door will be the opening
to my room. It will be like
a deer path through the meadow.

I remember when my skull was an abalone shell,
when my backbone was a flute.
Now there are seeds on my tongue, between my teeth.

HOLLY PRADO

THE MOUTH THAT IS A WOUND

huge
when she comes back to me
it is the dark this sea
cracks
bones
hang from her
arms around me I fight
my legs rise
she wants me I want
to sink with her to run

a child I threw stones
hurt myself on knives fire
she took that
loved me I was her
girl
then she lost
weight comfort
died
I stared
believed I was frozen in her
eyelids hair the same color the same
my own
mother

this has happened before
to everyone

I push to high ground
a place where I am not the girl with small bare teeth
I look toward the waves
light forms at the top of each one
others farther out
where is it
the moment you
the one time
you
feel the egg catch hold
when
does the face take shape

every month I search my blood for her
hungry
the myth of all animals
growing from one body

HOLLY PRADO

THE NIGHT YOU GOT BACK FROM THE MOUNTAINS

the dream is that you are half crow
feathers your shoulders
you think of flying across
how far
everything on the tree hangs slowly ripe

I wait behind moon and a few stars
carry an armload of peaches apricots
it is the waiting always the life that starts in a dark place
in my belly in my hair falls toward the ground
I catch what I can
turn into salt the hard core of an apple
seeds
become hills

I feel you around me coyote love
you howl with my breathing
the omens are lake and a sky

THE TROPICS

my own musk
late at night the huge red blossoms
droop over a wall
again my womb always my empty center
a stone in my hair in the mouth of my legs
the deep past
somewhere
I have set fires
their flames like hoods
clear breath cut from my ribs
whatever is growing is wild
whatever is dying groans

how do I say I am
so alone
how do I crouch
to give birth
my children my womb of fish gray silver curved
the shape of my hands that reach for them
in the river
struggling

DEL MARIE ROGERS

WAR REQUIEM

The restless water of sound,
a community of singers, one song,
one harsh voice,
the souls of the dead flow over our hands . . .

the fast pickup truck on a winter morning
is full of shaking branches, wet, piled high, precarious,
hanging out behind the truck,
cut off, hurtling forward in the cold sky.

IN THE MOUNTAIN CABIN

Waking close to the trees
in a cabin of rough wood
we can feel their presences.
Even before we are fully awake
our sleep goes branching upward in a lake of light.

When we are dead the trees will still
stand here asleep in the sun.
Listen, the light ticks quietly
on clean linen.
Rise, be well.

DESERT

In winter my mother goes away,
looking for missing dead, stones, ghosts that never stir the
        air.
The barking of dogs follows her into the vapor of sunrise.

I am learning the distances.
The stars are hard to see, she walks through crowds of
        people,
falling sand, rooms full of cold.

Birds rise over her shoulders,
a streak of blood.
On the horizon she lifts her hand to warn me.

DEL MARIE ROGERS

PHOTOGRAPH OF THE BACK OF MY HOUSE

Tracks in the snow
leading nowhere.

A row of lawn chairs, lined up
for Mommy and Daddy
and brother and sister
and bear and rabbit and baby
to view the sunset together,
and all of them empty.

Iron porch rail, cold steps,
closed shutters, miles through the snow,
and patience, patience,
miles of walking back.

RENÉE ROPER

EMMA IN MY THIRD EYE

skin of
    elm ebony eucalyptus
standing in gardens
with apples
snuffboxes hide in her branches
sunset eyes
    count her rings
    when she speaks
beauty worn from handwashing
in cracked black shoes
she looks in streetways
for blades of grass.

RENÉE ROPER

GOING HOME

They tell me she's crazy.
Wild Woman.
No one understands her.
Got a spot on her brain.
That makes her crazy.
      "We call it a blood clot."
Said it like I was a kid.
Think all niggers are crazy
or children.
All I want is to see her.
Make sure.

Saying she's dangerous.
We all are.
Just like locking us up.

She's always been wild.
Used to fight and loud on me
all the time.
Threw ten goddamn pounds of flour
on me once. It was summer.
And we laughed.
Shit, it was beautiful.
Flour all over.
Warm, sweated
white paste on her breasts.
Called us both crazy that day
but we were fine.
They just didn't know.

Threw me out once, too.
Cussed me out righteously.
Stayed out all night.
Threw my clothes down the stairs.
"Mad woman" "Serves you right"
"Woman, you a peck o'trouble."

But after she raised all that hell
I looked up from the street
raised my eyes to her and said
"Woman, is the LADY of the house in?"
and her laugh broke the night.

She got a temper, I'll admit.
She can act crazy sometimes
but she's o.k. If they'd just
let me see. Got to get her out.
Without me. Without her.
I don't know.

CANIBOLOS DE LA MONTANA
(A DIARY IN SIX PARTS)

We rode updrafts to Bolivia.

Curious, the Andes rush
trying to reach through crystal.

Then came a loud darkness.

  II
My lids scrape upwards;
white and gray
refilling the sockets.
Clouds focus as snow,
shredded steel, splattered glass.

Your black hair hid
the red paste and loose skin.

Locked in embrace
I told you of birds circling,
screaming in the distance.

It took three men
to break the lovers' knot.

(more)

III

The thirteenth night
a man I sat with
threw meat in the fire.
The shape was familiar.

IV

Removing wallets, clothing and rings
we tried not to think of it,
tried not to speak of it.

V

By the 60th day
the women I slept with
began to smell like you.
We had almost forgotten
there was a life before this
when the plane landed.

VI

The bones have been gathered.
Your family does not speak.
They do not know who you are.

PEGGY RUSE

A VISIT TO MY FATHER-IN-LAW ON MEMORIAL DAY

I picked some flowered weeds,
enough to stuff
an old can filled with creek water.

I cooled my feet burned
walking Road 80 to Newport.

I wish I had brought my bathing suit
or some poems
so I could loiter in the water,
sit under a tree
reading.

(more)

In California
for two years
I missed you laughing,
drinking with me,
telling Joe and me
what a good deal
you would give us
on grandma's house,
new lumber
you sawed ten years back.

The day you drank
vinegar
you swore
it was the best red wine
you ever tasted
including Thunderbird.
Good ole
rot-gut wine
should wash
your cement name,
instead of warm
sprinkler water
wetting dead grass.

Next year I'll come back with red grapes.

I thought
I would break
inside
from loving you alive.
I crack wide open.

PITTSBURGH

You lie in this Pittsburgh room
Full-length on the hotel sheets
Stiff with unloving, naked in the last light.
Sorrow hangs in this room like falling dust.

The window looks out to the business
Of the lost day, heavy with smog.
I search for a dark lake, a rising wind
Only to find a building burning, fifth avenue on fire.

No light in this night room
Gives away your hiding place
I wait for your voice
We winter this room with our cold mouths.

I remember coming to a Fort Bragg beach,
You and I finding the old sea lion dead
Its body hollowed out by ants and small crabs,
A carved hole where the heart had been.

VIEW OF VIENNA FROM SCHONBRUNN

Five o'clock closes in on another Sunday.
Dusk and bulb outline the Summer Palace
Baroque in the last sunlight.
The waterless fountains, loose of spray,
Mottled rust and green with moss.

I have come to this place, weary of Europe,
Resting my history at the feet of trojans,
Granite red in the sunset
Crying from dumb mouths.
I come to Vienna.

How beautiful the distant Danube is:
A motionless flowing, a silent split
Cutting Vienna in half.
Clouds by the naked sundown kindled
Unite, absorb, pull apart.

"The perpetual renovation of the city,
with its destruction of the pasts of individual men. . ."
I live, not durably
seeing all the pasts.
My gaze wanders from Vienna's and the world's.

I have seen the sea a hundred places in Europe,
I hear it shelled inside my ears.
The waves of Vienna wash me, hide me for this hour.
I smell salt, taste it on my mouth
Yet from where I sit I cannot see a coast.

Now a golden glass reflection, Schonbrunn
Stares back, waiting for the gates to close
On me who never knew history's chains;
I turn away from Vienna's light,
Pause to feel my way in the dark.

MARGARET RYAN

WHISTLER'S FATHER

George Washington Whistler, chief engineer
of the Trans-Siberian Railroad

You are rarely remembered, old man.
Your road of steel runs east, into the sun,
or to the sea, to Vladivostok, that most distant town.
But you are long gone, buried in the ground
you helped to tame. Steel rails cross
all continents. Some fall to rust. We ride
on giant silver planes and go
to Vladivostok rarely, if at all.

Your wife's well-known. The canvas
has not cracked or gone to dust.
"Arrangement Number One in Grey and Black"
still stands, or rather, hangs, a monument of sorts.
Year after year she sits there, staring
straight ahead at nothing we can see.
She does not move. The curtain hangs in folds.
Her hands are very white, and very old.

DREAMS OF EURYDICE

I

I want to leave him.
Again and again I walk out, into the meadow.
The women come with me.
Dressed in white tunics their hair
is fragrant with flowers.
I am happy with them.
We are all dancing.
I do not know him, I have never known him,
we have never been lovers.

II

We dance in a ring, holding hands.
The center is empty, except for flowers.
Blue ones, clinging like tears to the tall stalks,
white ones, circlets of lace
like the veil I was wearing.
I dance bare-headed now.
I have no distinction.
I am nobody's wife.
I am perfectly happy.

III

A sharp pain in my foot. Then
I am falling through darkness.
I think: *I am dead now,*
He cannot touch me.

The queen offers her gifts,
dark fruits heavy with sweetness.
We walk in the shadows or talk all day in the grasses.
I walk with a limp
and she tells me her secrets.

IV

His voice is light.
He is singing:
He loves me, oh, how he loves me.
And wants me back. I do not want
to go. I want to resist him.
I do not know him, I say.
I have never known him,
we have never been lovers.
No one will listen.

V

It is a stranger I follow,
a broad back covered with rags,
a lyre slung over one shoulder,
a man's body so large it blocks
the bright mouth of the cavern.
If he would turn, if I could see
his face—I call his name,
and he looks back.
Once more I am falling, or dancing.

VIRGINIA SCOTT

the president says . . .

the president says

eat fish

what is to be done . . .

what is to be done
to destroy this enemy?
what is to be done?
or must the entire system
f
  a
   l
    l
     ?
southeastasiachilemozambique
palestineangolaguineabissau
greecenow
the pattern is war

in countries colonized
by the West
how to do more than
merely stand up for the
               truth

what is to be done
to destroy this enemy?
what is to be done?

ELEGY

my mother in the witness box
witnessed for my sister burned alive
fought for her hard
while our opposition
argued that my mother
was not a fit substitute
for my sister
because she had terminal cancer
she was the grandmother
with cancer in her marrow
not long to live
still   she fought
in the witness box
angry
persistent
hopeful
understanding only part of
the issue

still   believing what she believed in
her oldest daughter dead at thirty-one
her granddaughters needing her
protection
she fought hard
in Salem Court House, Massachusetts

three months later
when we lost my sister's
daughters
my mother's ribs broke
as she cried

JUDITH SERIN

ORANGE TREE DREAM

This man who seems to be my husband
Has hundreds of orange trees
That smell all day
All day we wade through the smell
Our hands sticky with it
We hand each other words like spoonfuls of syrup
Oranges fall on the roof
Night fills up with their growing
Turning
The sudden decision to sever
Oranges roll down the stairs
Sit on our doorstep like kittens
And what we have between us
Is round and bright and could be opened into sections
Once I fell asleep on the porch
He covered me with orange blossoms

JUDITH SERIN

The sheep on these hills . . .

The sheep on these hills
Are not always the same sheep
Though indistinguishable
Like snow

My life
Will not remain
Frozen in this image

And I cannot fight the invisible
The snake who tensing his muscles in the grass
Looks exactly like the grass
Or hide on that day when one cell
May quietly start dividing
My body now an enemy

There is an immense isolation in pain
Where nobody wants to be
No matter how many have gone there
You must go by yourself

And I want so much to stay here
Shrinking in the sun
Animals breathing around me

A sock left by the road. . .

A sock left by the road
Fills with sunlight
A shed skin which begins its own life

Our leavings
Have the dignity of snails
Moving slowly into their surroundings

We cannot use them
They have turned toward the earth

They are not our houses

But when we walk
They call to us
Like baby seals washed up on shore

Who cannot swim
Who cannot live on land

There is a blue scarf
I picked up once in the rain

It took weeks to dry

It languishes in a drawer
Too small for any neck

LAYLE SILBERT

RELICTS

Is the slide
holding a section
of liver tissue
from Doctor Sun Yat-sen,
dead in 1925,
and preserved
by Yenching University
in Peking?

Are his cancerous cells
relict under glass
in the medical school
which sits among slopes and lakes
with benches and bicycle paths
on a green campus
mapped on a yellow old land?

Where are the wooden teeth
of President G. Washington
and what holy place
holds the prepuce of Jesus?

Gone the wallpaper that horrified
Oscar Wilde.

BREATHE IN BREATHE OUT

Not under a stone.
Let me take you in my arms,
your long bones hanging light and loose,
lay you on a pile of pleasant cut wood,
wrapped in white cloth
and turned to the vultures above,
your mouth black and open on your last words
and eyes sunk in their site.
Sad women in the burning ghat
will cover their heads
and a thousand hands shiver with fire,
burn your birth in Novgorod.
Consumed you enter the air.
Breathe in breathe out.

GOOD MORNING

Appreciate
the wide pavements
and silent people in nightclothes
watering their lawns—
an old party in a doorway
for his newspaper,
a woman opening hers in her robe.

They turn on the hour
like figures in the great clockwork
of Frankfurt
this morning in Los Angeles
out of houses in rows
dropped down the street,
pieces facing on a board.

DALENE STOWE

MUSCLE BUILDING

1

Every day I work a little on my biceps.
All my life I've been led to believe
I had weak arms.
Men have said, you have strong feet,
Strong legs, gluttials, sphincter, cunt:
Like a serpent, you can coil.
The male eye tells me I have power
From the waist down.
When it comes to handling things
I am armless, fixed to the earth.
There are limits as to
What I can carry,
What I can shape,
What I can join.
Like an intense color I am rooted to one place.
My strength has always consisted of tenacity:
From the waist down.

2

Today I have another idea.
I picture a woman with a copper voice;
The weaver, the beater of flax,
The crusher of wheat and berries;
The corn grinder,
The woman who was pushing rocks;
The woman who had the wings of an eagle,
And whose business it was to tread air like water;
The woman who kneaded the clouds like dough,
Who broke a thick sky loaf over deserts of clay and fiber,
Who stirred a sky flood with magnificent arms
And stopped it with the smooth wall of her shoulder;
The woman with the oak clavicle and elbows of turf and
    shadow;
The woman whose forearms were towers and whose
    bones were bridges;
Bridges to what?

3

I shall build you a rampart
For your carvings of pearwood.
I shall shelter your intricate inlays,
Your lute of a thousand seeds and sexes,
Your cup of a thousand bloods.
I shall surround the labyrinth of your heart
With red tile and blue stone;
I shall build for you a stairway of flesh and window,
A spiral of energy
On which you can climb, dance,
And draw things to you.
On which you can construct,
With your own arms,
A center.

DALENE STOWE

DAY TIME SEQUENCE/NOVEMBER

The wind has no voice, really.
The obstacles have voices.
Going up hill
This crow time of year
The cartilage cracks,
The wind announces:
November is the month of cartilage.
Small bones
All over your body applaud.

But the wind has no voice, really.
It is the obstacles that have announced it.
Once in life
Something like November happens in the body:
The joints are exposed.
Twigs grinding in upon themselves
Produce the voices you thought were the breath.

The crow is blood, this time,
Covering your nakedness
With a harsh name. Obstacles.
Like light jarring off a coin
Winter approaches your spinal column.
The small bones in your wrists and ankles
Are no longer intricate maps,
Ready to take you anywhere.

POEM TO MY TWIN POSSIBILITY

My house was an infinite series of houses;
I was known by an infinite series of names.
When I woke up, everywhere I saw colored plates;
I fixed breakfast in a corridor of mirrors;
I dreamed in double vision and heard bravos.

Every year I purposefully forgot Mother's Day,
That river of alternatives.
I also forgot the rose of your double deadly birthday,
The telephone book with your number in it,
Battered by snow.

You were the baffler, energy.
You were the locomotive, awareness.
You were the loved one of infinite names,
My twin possibility.

Your life was a series of bravos,
And you were a real record-breaker,
The groove in my golden record heart.

I was prepared to die the death
Of the love of objects
But you stopped me with a written test
(bravo)
You had a soft, straight back,
And a voice that would split into colors
Through the prism of a phone call.

You had a laugh like a stilletto
And a skeleton like a lace tablecloth:
You were my ideal.
And I, in the apex of my convalescence,
Loved you   (bravo)

And I, in the apex of my convalescence,
Loved you   (bravo)

MARY SWANSON STROH

THE FARMER'S WIFE

I could tell you
about the windows full
of breeding thickets and trees,
about the cottonwood seeds
clinging to the screens
but that is not enough.

Follow me
and watch my moist breath
crown the heavy air;
find with me
the relief of a bed.
Because everyone and everything
has gone out into the night
I can lie here
never once blinking cover
for my hard black eyes.

EXCUSES

The Italian women in the back room
have stood since the depression
cutting fettucini, nodding scarved heads:
"family is family"
"sick is sick."
I want you to be that simple.
I don't want to walk with you
the night's too much codeine
cracks your head on the toilet.
Some part of you comes to me, only this time
it is my fingers that twist through your gray hair—
banging your head against the wall.
Mother, my arms are not soft enough, my breasts
not large enough to fold you in
and stroke out your bitterness.
We sift through our separate stacks
of dirty dishes, ashtrays, books; substitute
coffee for speech, pry open black windows
wishing it were spring, and wonder
why it is so difficult not to be a man.

MARY SWANSON STROH

NOVEMBER BIRTHDAY

The mist came up thick this morning,
nearly fog, covering the stars and sunrise.
Later, in town, smoke from the power plant
is caught in it: stretched out across the river
not rising, not sinking, only stretching

more and more thin.
The wetness settles, covering faces.
Condemned storefronts just stand there,
their backs half eaten by odd teeth and cranes:
toilets and radiators hang crazed
at the sudden rush of space.
There is nothing to say. There are only falling bricks.

They would light the ward at dusk.
Whoever I was, then, watched out the window
and held your small bruised head against my breast,
felt the newness of your mouth pull and suck
and slacken into sleep.
So, we laid there,
and I watched out
glad for the dark and wet streets.

LIBERATION (a love poem)

Always there is this crossing
and recrossing of life.
I have started this poem many times,
coming up to the city
from the Randolph St. Station
the old man in the alley was a hero
selling dyed carnations, his secret fame.

I remember cone-shaped worlds of light
stretching from streetlamps to the asphalt
and see the whiteness of a maternity ward,
two nurses bent over my empty belly
kneading out the useless blood.

The night we drove on through mountains
and the salt flats, then more mountains,
there was time, there was time
while all the world was hidden in the dark
to have noticed something more
than the climbing and twisting of the road.
Nothing ever gets said,
especially when there's time.
Still, I was writing this poem.

What is it that I want?
To reach out of my body before it dies.
I want to stretch out my hands
and watch the rising moons on my fingertips
become transparent—
I want to believe it is possible to touch
past layers of skin and veins—
that I won't have to die in here, alone.

KAREN WHITEHILL

MAGDALENE, AFTERWARD

She dreams of the desert again
running after him, stumbling in sand
he glances back over his shoulder
Noli me tangere

Outcast
she still follows
      the devil is in her again

Shaking his head
he reminds her the path
long and hard
leads away from the world

He explains how he hated the city,
the shapes of disgust in the fair

She recalls how the ropes of her hair
fit his feet like a sandal

how he looked at her eyes
as if he'd found water

Well   she reflects
Who would know he had risen
if I hadn't come

She awakes with wet palms
bitter salt on her tongue

How she wanted to make it
a pilgrimage!
He was her sole
high priest of beauty
each footprint a blessing

Was it the sun
radiant on his forehead
that made him seem a prophet?
Or the stone
glaring in the distance
that blinds her to other men?

What kind of marriage was this?
What kind of mirage?

Now
with heaven and earth between them
a potent thought
malleable as her flesh

remains

KAREN WHITEHILL

PENELOPE

Odysseus,
once I was ready to split
the tree-carved bed
you were so proud of
into firewood

now it's hard to remember
how I burned those first years

time goes by and I neglect
to look after your arms
the bows all unstrung

the house is a wreck
suitors multiply like flies
what can I do but spin
edging my borders?

my life is preparation only
I forget whether I wait
to see you again
or to see this embroidery complete

so I elaborate
spend all my days
here in this high
lonely room
bemused

the needle eyes me
like some enchanted god

the pattern absorbs me
what began as a cover
has gotten so complicated

each night it gets harder
to unravel it all

my fingers tremble
at this material
I keep losing the thread

one seam
leads to another

see
the design is a woman
weeping inconsolably

for her husband

MORNING IN GAINESVILLE

Here the whitest birds
learn to stalk cattle for flies

Against the brilliant hard sky
clouds billow and drift
like sheets hung up to dry

Wandering in fields
students gather magic
mushrooms sprung up after rain

Black lovebugs are all over now
stuck together in twos
sucked into every closing door

In the distance
the skeleton of a live oak
licked clean by beards of moss
gleams in the sun

MARTHA YOAK

SUNDAY EVENING WITH ELIZABETH, AGE 5

The moon is balking its bleached skin from the November
    night.
No light lowers, and the clouds clip their way over the
    black trees.
I keep my vigil at your window as the night birds call each
    other
From the leaves. It's more than a revel for them, and
Hungrily, they wait—the purposed wings wrapped about
    them,
Eyes glittering like wet worms.

Enshrouded in your bed, you sleep a kind sleep.
The moon banks over the roof, one bright edge arching its
    cyclops' eye.

The clouds trough and whirl, then scud reluctantly to let
  one
Star through.

This morning we were chased from the church like
  vampires—
The cross they waved still dances polished and discreet.
Now, I wait this night as you sleep; I wait and watch for
  the birds to come,
Batting their blind way to your heart and the warm pool of
Blood pulsing there like a rose.
Church, Elizabeth. Your first time there, and it was I who
  led
You into that place; this cuckolded shepherd let you up to
  the
Slow beat of the organ note and the echoing voice.

The birds are performing a black masque—the bats, the
  ravens, the dowager
Crows have all succumbed to their deacons' habits. They
  nibble lice
From each other like crumbs and propel their feathers into
  the night like scaly black ribbons.
It is their church: they wait as
Patient as father confessors—and they wait hungry.

I wait at your window for their mock burial to end, for the
Crusade to begin.
I would wait here until the sun comes up like a search light
  and
Shreds their wings with its fire.
I am waiting with my catacombed shell of a heart, hoping
  that though
They come in a vast howling cloud in the night,
I will be brave, and
This kindness let you sleep.

MARTHA YOAK

MOTHER AND I

After these thirty years, Mother,
I am almost as old now as you were when
You grew me
In your greenhouse beneath your apron—
That small toy that emerged with the flood,
Waxy-boned, tiny muscles tied on like strawberries,
Yet sturdy as a coaster wagon.

If you had counted my first breath's whimper a fearful
    thing,
And refused to curl my palm in yours;
If my foot had not been helped to step out of your bone
    into my bone,
Then it would have been light lost from my eyes.
But you kept me in your hands.

Now that I'm at the age where
I see the intimacy of the clock as ours too,
And see the possibility of its running down,
I try to know you, and find
You are as distinct from me now as I from my watery
    beginning.

MOTHER AND THE MOON

The sky droops like the lapel on a corpse
As we wait this night together.
    Your fear, Mother, and
    My love are beyond you.

Inside looms the first cell—
    A moon open as an autopsy,
    A mouth that clamps down its own tongue.

Why were you pretty, Mother,
And why did you laugh?
You danced spring awake, your breath flying like
    hummingbirds.

Then it was your father who gaffed your heart with his
    hook and
Hung you up to bleed.

The black holes of space, immobile and seized,
Smoke midnight to a coma.

We wait cold in the field:
At the house the wood fire burns with a blue heat,
    Warming a man who has learned how to survive.
    His hand arches his Bible like a scorpion's tail.

Light pivots on the horizon, slumps back into space.

PAULETTE DUSDALL ZACHARIOU

STICKS AND STONES

I am listening to the silence
between the voices
of the children
and I am living in my bones
as I've never done before.
Skeletal.
I move my hips, my jaw.
This flesh melts so easily
a pound off my arms,
a closer look at the core,
the shape, the form beneath
that craves dancing
as much as embrace.

PAULETTE DUSDALL ZACHARIOU

IN THE MORNING

The salted chips
were not enough,
nor the fresh guacamole
with the light red wine.

In the morning, walking
down Geary Street, peering
into gift shops, squinting
in the glare, I saw someone.
And just the way he hurried by
left me standing, wanting you

to hear the grinding of the bus
and to feel the hot air of the exhaust,
to smell the ten a.m. flavor
of donut, coffee, puddles from last night's rain
with me.
I turn back to the shops seeing
shelves of china cups, glittering
crystal ashtrays, molded metal
flying cranes.

IN THE EMBERS AT MIDNIGHT

Indian riding
a house down waves
turn.
I follow and your feathers
flow into other
riderless horses.

Ahead a long pathway.
At the end
a small green door.
A hand
or spider
comes out.

I meet a fox with peacock feathers,
abalone like, see other Indian feathers
on a headdress
or a wing. I'm looking.
There is a man
crawling
underneath a bearskin.

"On the Border of Impossibility" and "Sunday" copyright 1975 by Laura Beausoleil.

"Night of Dreams" by Laura Beausoleil was first published in *Strange Faeces* #15, 1974.

"Becket" by Virginia Gilbert copyright 1969 by *Lyrical Iowa*. "Pax Romana" by Virginia Gilbert first appeared in *Sumac*.

"Mother Your Children Give You. . ." by Karen L. Kent was first published in *The Lamp in the Spine*, Fall/Winter 1973–74.

"Dreams from War" by Marilyn Krysl first appeared in the *Seneca Review*, May 1973, copyright *Seneca Review*, 1973.

"Alchemy" by Diane Levenberg first appeared in *Response*, Spring 1973.

"Out of the Desert" by Diane Levenberg copyright 1975 by *Earth's Daughters*, #5–6.

"each night. . ." "i am riding a lion. . .," "Weather Report," and "There Is No Time," copyright 1975 Elaine H. Jennings.

"Misericordia" by Teresa A. McCarthy first appeared in *Windmill*, 1974.

"Letter to Belden" by Rosalie Moore was first published in *Southern Poetry Review*, Spring 1974.

"Brother at One Week" by Carole Oles first appeared in *Yes (A Magazine of Poetry)*, Winter 1974.

"There Was a Time," by Gerrye Payne first appeared in *Loon* #1, 1973.

"The Night You Got Back from the Mountains" by Holly Prado first appeared in *Specimen*, 1973.

"The Tropics," by Holly Prado first appeared in *California State Poetry Quarterly*, Los Angeles, Winter 1974.

"Desert" by Del Marie Rogers first appeared in *The New Salt Creek Reader* copyright 1973 by Windflower Press.

"In the Mountain Cabin" by Del Marie Rogers first appeared in *I Had Been Hungry All the Years* copyright 1975.

"Photograph of the Back of My House" by Del Marie Rogers first appeared in *Kayak 10*, 1973.

"Pittsburgh" by Peggy Ruse was first published in *Aisling*, Summer 1974, copyright 1974 by Paul Shuttleworth.

"Dreams of Eurydice" by Margaret Ryan first appeared in *Syracuse Poems 1974* copyright Dept. of English, Syracuse University, 1974.

"Whistler's Father" copyright 1975 by Margaret Ryan.

"The President Says. . .," "What Is to Be Done. . ." and "Elegy" copyright 1975 by Virginia Scott.

"The Sheep on these Hills" by Judith Serin first appeared in *Transfer*, Fall 1974.

BIOGRAPHICAL NOTES

LAURA BEAUSOLEIL was born October 1, 1948, in Willits, California, and reared on an Oregon farm. She received an M.A. from San Francisco State University where she worked with Nanos Valaoritis. Her poetry and collages have appeared in *Bastard Angel, 14 Voices, Heirs, Kayak, Strange Faeces,* and in *Autograph,* a chapbook. Ms. Beausoleil, the mother of one child, lives in San Francisco.

JOANNE CASULLO, born July 24, 1949, in Manhattan, spent her childhood years in Queens. She earned her B.A. at Syracuse University, her M.F.A. at University of Iowa. She has worked with Marvin Bell, Philip Booth, Donald Justice, W.D. Snodgrass, and Mark Strand. She is married and lives in Colorado Springs.

DELIA CHILGREN was born June 11, 1948, and raised in San Francisco. She received her B.A. from San Francisco State University and J.D. from Golden Gate University Law School. She has given readings for Poetry-in-the-Schools and the San Francisco Public Library. Her poetry has appeared in *Aisling, Way Poems,* and *Wayfaring.* A coeditor of *Wayfaring* and former associate editor of the G.G.U. *Law Review,* she is currently a practicing attorney in San Francisco.

CATHY COLMAN, born June 16, 1951, in New York City, grew up on Long Island and in Los Angeles. She attended the University of California at Berkeley and received her B.A. from San Francisco State University where she is now doing graduate work. In 1974 she was a winner of San Francisco State's Browning Award for poetry. Formerly a women's studies teacher, she has given readings at Intersection, The Owl & Monkey, and at the Oakland Museum. She resides in Berkeley, California.

ELLEN COONEY was born in St. Louis, June 23, 1948. Her childhood was spent in St. Louis and Montclair, New Jersey. She earned her B.A. at Lone Mountain College in San Francisco and did graduate study at San Francisco State University. She has worked with Diane di Prima, Mark Linenthal, Stan Rice, Nanos Valaoritis, and has given readings at the San Francisco Zen Center, and Lone Mountain College. Her work has been published in *Aisling, Amazon Quarterly, Gay Sunshine, Evergreen Review, Libera, Poetry Pageant, Prism International, St. Ignatius Bulletin.* She lives in San Francisco.

TOI DERRICOTTE was born April 12, 1941, in Detroit where she spent her childhood. Currently a graduate student at New York University, she studied at Cooper Union, New School for Social Research, and at Wayne State University where she earned her B.A. She worked with William Packard and has been published in *New York Quarterly.* Her awards include first prize in the 1974 N.Y.U. Academy of American Poets Competition, the Pen and Brush Award from New School for Social Research, and a Poetry and Art Prize from Englewod Cliffs College. A poetry workshop teacher, Ms. Derricotte is married and resides in Montclair, New Jersey.

KATHERINE DOAK was born in Northampton, Massachusetts, January 25, 1952. She was reared in upstate New York and in Vermont. She studied at the University of

Alaska and Smith College, and has worked with John Haines. She currently lives outside Fairbanks, Alaska.

CLAUDIA DOBKINS, born October 4, 1949, spent her childhood in rural and suburban Indianapolis. She received her A.A. from Northwood of Indiana, and studied at Herbert Berghof Studio. She has worked with Barbara Holland and Deborah Richardson, and has given readings at Basement Coffee House, Loeb Student Center, New York Poets' Cooperative, St. Marks in the Bowery. Her work has been published in *Best in Poetry, Dasein,* and *Stone Soup.* Formerly a teacher at University of the Street in New York, she is currently on the staff of *New York Quarterly.* She lives in New York City.

VIRGINIA GILBERT was born December 19, 1946, in Elgin, Illinois, and spent her childhood in Cary, Illinois. She received her B.A. from Iowa Wesleyan College, her M.F.A. from University of Iowa, and her Ph.D. from University of Utah. She has worked with Marvin Bell, Kathleen Fraser, Galway Kinnell, and George Starbuck. Her poetry has appeared in *Back Door, Beloit Poetry Journal, Crazy Horse, Laureate, New Voices in American Poetry, Prairie Schooner, Quetzal, Seneca Review, Sumac.* Formerly a Peace Corps teacher in Korea, she now teaches college and lives in Salt Lake City.

ELLEN McEVILLEY GRIFFIN was born in Cincinnatti, August 26, 1937, and grew up in the Cincinnatti suburbs. She received her B.A. from Wellesley College, M.S.W. from Fordham School of Social Work, and an M.A. from the University of

Florida. She has worked with Philip Booth and Adrienne Rich, and been published in the *Wellesley Literary Quarterly.* Formerly a psychiatric social worker, she currently writes psychosocial evaluations. She is married, has one child, and lives in Gainesville, Florida.

ELIZABETH HANSON was born June 30, 1952, in Plymouth, Massachussetts; her childhood was spent in Bristol, Rhode Island. She received her B.A. from Roger Williams College, her M.A. from University of Massachussetts. She has worked with Donald Justice, Joseph Langland, William Mathews, and Franklin Zawacki. Her poetry has appeared in *The Goodly Co.* and *Aldebaran.* She has worked as a clerk, secretary, and cashier, and currently resides in Amherst, Massachusetts.

PATRICIA HENLEY was born in 1947 in Terre Haute, Indiana, where she spent her childhood. Her work has been published in *New Salt Creek Reader, Southern Review, Three Rivers Poetry Journal,* and in a chapbook, *Fever Feast.* She was formerly Poet-in-Residence of the South Carolina Arts Commission, and is currently editor of Peace Weed Press. She is married, has one child, and lives in Davenport, Washington.

ELAINE JENNINGS was born December 1, 1945, in Norwood, Massachusetts. She grew up in rural New Jersey, and received her A.A. from Monmouth College. She has been published in *Dekalb Poetry Review, The Fiddlehead, Hyacinths & Biscuits, Monmouth Letters, Out of Sight, Poet Lore, Poetry Venture, West Coast Poetry Review,* and others, including a chapbook, *A Bird Sliding Noise.* In 1971, she won first place in the Mississippi Poetry Contest. Formerly a journalist, she is married, has three children, and lives in Sacramento, California.

KAREN KENT was born May 1941, and raised in rural Iowa. She received her M.A. and M.F.A. from University of Iowa. Her poetry will be published in a forthcoming book, *I Look Good*. She has two children and lives in Iowa City, Iowa.

GLORIA KOSTER was born December 28, 1950, in Plainfield, New Jersey, where she spent her childhood. She studied at New School for Social Research, New York University, receiving her B.A. from Bennington College, and her M.S. from Hofstra University. She has worked with Michael Dennis Browne and Richard Ellman. Currently a junior high school teacher, she is married and lives in Scarsdale, New York.

MARILYN KRYSL, born in 1942, was raised in Eugene, Oregon, and Sylvan Grove, Kansas. She has an M.F.A. from the University of Oregon. Her poetry and prose have been published in *Atlantic, Best Little Magazine Fiction–1971, December, Iowa Review, Massachusetts Review, New Republic, Northwest Review, Seneca Review,* and others; a forthcoming book will be titled *Saying Things*. She won a grant from National Endowment for the Arts in 1974. She is the mother of one child, and currently teaches college in Boulder, Colorado.

DIANE LEVENBERG is currently a Ph.D. candidate and working as a teacher in New York City. Her poetry has appeared in *Aphra,*

Earth's Daughters, Jewish Spectator, New York Quarterly, and *Response*.

MARY L. LOGUE was born in St. Paul, Minnesota, April 16, 1952; she was raised in the St. Paul suburbs. She studied at Université d'Aix-Marseille and received her B.A. from the University of Minnesota. She has worked with Michael D. Browne and James Moore. Her poetry has been published in *Dakota Territory, Moons and Lions Tails, Preview, Thrush, Wisconsin Review*. In 1974 she was awarded first prize in the University of Minnesota Academy of American Poets Competition. Formerly a freelance writer, she now works as a magazine editor in St. Paul.

KATHLEEN LUBECK was born January 20, 1950, in Berkeley, California, and grew up in the San Francisco Bay Area. She received her B.A. and M.A. from Brigham Young University. Formerly a college instructor, she is now a journalist in Provo, Utah.

TERESA McCARTHY, born in 1944 in Hays, Kansas, grew up in Indiana and Oklahoma. Currently an M.A. candidate at University of Oklahoma, she has worked with Robert Bly and Kenneth Koch. Her work has appeared in *Windmill*. Formerly a teacher, she is a staff member of *Windmill*. She is married, has one child and lives in Norman, Oklahoma.

NANCY MAIRS was born July 23, 1943, in Wenham, Massachusetts, where she spent her childhood. She received her B.A. from Wheaton College, and is currently working on an M.F.A. at University of Arizona. She has worked with Jean Pedrick and Richard Shelton, and given readings at Cambridge Street Artists' Cooperative, University of Arizona, and in high schools. Her poems have appeared in *Arion's Dolphin* and *The Little Magazine*. Formerly a technical editor and staff member of *At the Gallery: An Anthology of Readings from the Cambridge Street Artists' Cooperative*, she is a college instructor. She is married, has two children, and lives in Tucson, Arizona.

POLLY MANN, born November 19, 1919, in Lenoke, Arkansas, grew up in Hot Springs, Arkansas. She studied at Mankato State College and Southwest Minnesota State College; worked with Phil Dacey and Helen Rezatto; and is published in *Changes, The Great Plains Observer, Perceptions, SWAFA News, Win, The Writer*. Formerly a journalist and secretary, she is a member of a traveling puppet troupe. She is married, a mother, and lives in Marshall, Minnesota.

ADRIANNE MARCUS, born March 3, 1935, in Everett, Massachusetts, was reared in Fayetteville, North Carolina. She attended Shorter College and received her B.A. and M.A. from San Francisco State University. In 1968 she was awarded a fellowship by the National Endowment for the Arts. Her work has been chosen twice by Borestone Mountain Best Poetry Publications; she was a Yaddo resident in 1973 and 1975. Her poetry has appeared in *Appalachian Review, Atlantic Monthly, Choice, Nation, Peace and Pieces, Poetry Northwest, Southern Poetry Review*, and others, and in a collection, *The Moon is a Marrying Eye*. She authored

the text for *The Photojournalist: Mary Ellen Mark & Annie Leibovitz*. Married and the mother of three children, Ms. Marcus is a college teacher and journalist residing in San Rafael, California.

MARY MOORE was born November 14, 1945, in Pasadena and spent her childhood in Orange County, California. She earned her B.A. at the University of California, Riverside, and is now studying for an M.A. at California State College at Sonoma. She has given readings at Santa Rosa Junior College; her poetry has appeared in *Aisling* and *Loon*. Formerly a social worker, she is married, has one child, and lives in Napa, California.

ROSALIE MOORE, born in Oakland, California, October 10, 1910, grew up in Alameda, California. She received her B.A. and M.A. from University of California, Berkeley. In 1949 she received the Yale Series Younger Poet Award for her collection, *The Grasshopper's Man*. She has been the recipient of two Guggenheim Fellowships and of the Vachel Lindsay Award from *Poetry;* she has won the First and Second Awards of the Year from the Poetry Society of America. Her work has appeared in *Accent, Furioso, The Golden Treasury of Poetry, The New Yorker, 100 Best Modern Poems, Saturday Review*, among others. Her forthcoming book is titled *Year of the Children*. A journalist and co-author of children's books, she currently chairs a college communications department. Married and the mother of three children, she lives in Larkspur, California.

BIOGRAPHICAL NOTES

RUBEE DREHER MOXLEY was born June 29, 1934, and reared in Louisville, Kentucky. She is now studying for the M.S.W. at Kent School of Social Work. Her poetry has appeared in *Anthology of the Angels, Black Scene Magazine,* and in *Greenup County News;* she has worked with Lee Pennington. Formerly a laboratory technician, she is an actress in community theater. Married and the mother of two children, she lives in Louisville.

CAROLE OLES was born in New York City on January 7, 1939; she grew up in Astoria and the Queens. She received her B.A. from Queens College in Flushing, and an M.A. from the University of California at Berkeley. She has worked with Maxine Kumin, Anne Sexton, and Kathleen Spivack; in 1974 she received a scholar award from Bread Loaf Writers' Conference and her work chosen for the *Borestone Anthology* of 1973. Her poetry has been published in *The Chowder Review, The Lyric, The New Salt Creek Reader, Prairie Schooner, Second Wave, 13th Moon, Twigs, Yes (A Magazine of Poetry),* and others. Formerly a teacher, publicist, textbook editor, she is currently a journalist. She is married, has two children, and lives in Newton, Massachusetts.

GERRYE PAYNE was born January 20, 1942, in Dallas, Texas. Her childhood was spent in Sacramento, California. She received her B.A. from the University of California at Berkeley, and is now working on an M.A. at California State College at Sonoma. Her work has appeared in *Aphra, Loon, Rolling Stone, Woman, Portrait, Reflection.* Currently she is an artist, a freelance writer, and college teacher. The mother of two children, she lives in Sebastopol, California.

HOLLY PRADO, born May 2, 1938, was reared in Nebraska and Michigan. She received her B.A. from Albion College and her teaching credential from California State University at Los Angeles. She has worked with Alvaro Cardona-Hine; has given readings at the Bodhi Tree, Chatterton's Book Shop, Evergreen Theater, Immaculate Heart College, KPFK Radio, Poetry Center at San Francisco State University, University of California at Irvine, and at the Venice Public Library. Her work has appeared in *Anthology of Los Angeles Poets, Apple, California State Poetry Quarterly, Chelsea, Lamp in the Spine, Open Spaces, Rolling Stone, Specimen '73, American Poetry Review.* She has worked as a master poet-teacher with Poetry-in-the-Schools, as a secretary, and a high school teacher. The editor of *Camera Ready,* an anthology of high school poetry, she currently teaches writing workshops in Los Angeles.

DEL MARIE ROGERS was born in Washington, D.C., April 11, 1936; she was reared in Dallas, Texas. She received her B.A. from Baylor University and her M.A. from Vanderbilt where she is a candidate for her Ph.D. Her awards include the National Endowment for the Arts in 1974 and a Danforth Fellowship from Vanderbilt University. She has given readings at the First Unitarian Church of San Antonio, Southern Methodist University, and at Trinity University. Her poetry and reviews have been published in *The Blackbird*

BIOGRAPHICAL NOTES

Circle, Carolina Quarterly, Changes, Choice, Epoch, Folio, Ironwood, Kayak, Measure, The Nation, Raleigh *News and Observer, Perspective, The Seventies,* and *Southern Poetry Review,* and others. She has been a high school and college instructor, director of an Upward Bound Program, and consultant to experimental schools. She is poetry editor of *Café Solo,* and coeditor of the anthology *I Had Been Hungry All These Years.* She is the mother of three children, and lives in Richardson, Texas.

RENÉE ROPER, born in Suffolk, Virginia, May 10, 1951, grew up in the Hotel Albert in Greenwich Village. She received a B.A. from the University of Bridgeport, and an M.F.A. from Columbia University. She has worked with Richard Brickner, Daniel Halpern, Galway Kinnell, Carolyn Kizer, and Norman Pritchard; she has given poetry readings at Bennington College, Cubiculo Theatre, Dr. Generosity's Poetry Pub, among others. Her writing has appeared in *Abbey Magazine, The Columbia Reader, Everywoman Magazine, Journal of Black Poetry.* Formerly a teacher in the Upward Bound Program. Ms. Roper is now a filmmaker and photographer in New York City.

PEGGY RUSE was born in San Francisco, October 4, 1949, and raised in San Rafael and Mill Valley, California. She studied at the College of Marin and Eastern Washington State and received her B.A. and M.A. from San Francisco State University. She has worked with Robert Haas, William Dickey, John Logan, James McAuley, Adrianne Marcus, and Phyllis Thompson; her poetry has

been published in *Aisling* and *Transfer.* She currently resides in San Francisco, California.

MARGARET RYAN was born in 1950 in Trenton, New Jersey, where she spent her childhood. She received her B.A. from the University of Pennsylvania and her M.A. from Syracuse University. She has worked with Philip Booth, George P. Elliot, Daniel Hoffman, and G.W. Meyers. She was awarded first place in the *Mademoiselle* College Poetry Competition of 1971; her poetry has been published in *Anchor Anthology, Intro 6,* and *Mademoiselle.* Formerly a teaching assistant, she now works for an advertising agency in New York City.

VIRGINIA SCOTT was born February 19, 1938, in Medford, Massachusetts, where she grew up. She received her B.A. from Boston University, her M.A. from University of Wisconsin, and Ph.D. at the City University of New York. She worked with Germaine Bill; her writings have been published in *City University Guide for the Teaching of College English, Connections, Jazz & Pop, Outside the Net, Pan-African Journal, Sunbury, West End,* and in a collection, *Poems for a Friend in Late Winter.* She is the owner of the Sunbury Press, the editor of *Sunbury: A Poetry Magazine,* a member of Coalition of Labor Union Women, and a college teacher in Bronx, New York.

JUDITH SERIN was born in New Jersey, May 16, 1949; she spent her childhood in Piscataway Township, New Jersey. She earned her B.A. at Bennington College and her M.A. at San Francisco State University. She

BIOGRAPHICAL NOTES

has worked with Michael Dennis Browne, Kathleen Fraser, Stan Rice, and given readings at San Francisco State University and Intersection. Her poetry has appeared in *The Real World* and *Transfer*. She is the author of a children's book, translator and stage adaptor of *Les Chantes de Maldoror*. She teaches adult education and lives in Berkeley, California.

LAYLE SILBERT, born in Chicago, earned her B.A. and M.A. degrees from the University of Chicago. Her poetry, prose, and articles have been published in *American Statistician, China Weekly Review, Congress Weekly, Chicago Defender, Shanghai Post & Mercury, The Villager, Group '74* and others. Her photography has appeared in *Contemporary Poetry in America, New York Quarterly, Rising Tides,* and in a one-person show in Quito, Ecuador. Formerly a freelance copy editor and a social worker, she is a staff member of *New York Quarterly.* She is married and lives in New York City.

DALENE STOWE, born in Long Beach, September 18, 1946, spent her childhood in southern California. She received her B.A. from California State University at Long Beach and an M.A. from the University of New York at Stony Brook where she is currently a candidate for her Ph.D. She has given readings at the University of New York at Stony Brook and in various communities; her poetry has been published in *Soundings* and *Voices.* Formerly a dancer with the Gloria Newman Modern Dance Company, she now teaches dance and hatha yoga, and heads a women's collective. She lives in Port Jefferson, New York.

MARY STROH was born in Chicago, April 4, 1949, and raised in Park Forest, Illinois. She studied at Southern Illinois University at Carbondale, and received her B.A. from the University of Iowa. She has worked with Marvin Bell, Norman Dubie, Larry Levis, Michael Ryan, and has given readings at the Iowa City Arts Cooperative. She is the mother of one child, and lives in Iowa City, Iowa.

KAREN WHITEHILL was born in Boston, September 1, 1947, and grew up in Reading, Massachusetts. She received her B.A. from Middlebury College and her M.A. from the University of Virginia. Formerly an editorial worker, she is married, the mother of one child, and lives in Charlottesville, Virginia.

MARTHA YOAK was born in Barbourville, West Virginia, December 17, 1942, and was raised in Avoca, Iowa, and West Virginia. She received her B.A., M.A., Ed.S. from the University of Iowa. She is a winner of the Carl Steiffel Memorial Award, and has been published in *Lyrical Iowa.* She has worked as an editorial assistant and a secretary; currently she is a college teacher. She lives in Keokuk, Iowa.

PAULETTE D. ZACHARIOU was born in San Francisco in 1943 and spent her childhood there. She received her B.A. from San Francisco State University. She is the mother of two children and lives in San Bruno, California.